The Crow's Collection Anthology

World Magic

A curated collection of articles offering perspectives on magical practice from around the world

Paperback ISBN: 978-1-964537-56-6
eBook ISBN: 978-1-968185-46-6

Library of Congress Control Number on file.

Published by:
Crossed Crow Books, LLC
518 Davis St, Suite 205
Evanston, IL 60201
www.crossedcrowbooks.com

Printed in the United States of America.
IBI

The Crow's Collection Anthology
World Magic
A curated collection of articles offering perspectives on magical practice from around the world

Chicago, IL

Table of Contents

Note from the Publisher

The world is full of magic. In spite of this, discourse on magical practices tends to narrowly focus on western and European expressions of occultism and witchcraft. Though the conversation is changing, magic is primarily defined by this Eurocentric (and often privileged) perspective. It is a loaded term carrying centuries of baggage, suppression, and colonial dismissal, among other things. This results in a limited and sometimes oppressive scope of what magic is and isn't. What's left out is an enormous range of living magical traditions that have persisted across cultures and continents, many of which may or may not even use the word "magic."

The Crow's Collection Anthology: World Magic offers a glimpse into practices that rarely appear in mainstream occult literature. The anthology is by no means comprehensive; our hope and goal is to open the conversation and encourage our dear readers to foster a deeper appreciation and awareness for myriad expressions of spirituality. It is a collection of individuals speaking to their practices, beliefs, and understandings. In it, we hear from the voices of both practitioners and academics, offering insights on everything from new translations of medieval Islamic texts and firsthand accounts of Mayan spirituality to the magic of the Balkans and Finnish folk magic. Some contributors are published for the first time; others are well-known writers within their field. Across the spectrum, they are all brilliant and insightful individuals.

We're grateful to each author for sharing their traditions and insights and for contributing to what we hope becomes a much larger conversation about amplifying silenced voices.

With the deepest gratitude,

—Blake & Gianluca, Crossed Crow Books

Everyone's Got a Haunted Barn

Ozark Daemonology in Practice

by Brandon Weston

Jim contacted me through a messenger app.

JIM: NEED HELP WITH GHOST

I couldn't tell if the capitalization meant this was an urgent situation or if he was just of a certain generation who leaves the caps lock on indefinitely. His next message was even more cryptic.

JIM: ITS IN A BARN

The Ozark Mountains have no shortage of old barns and ghosts. One old timer I know always says that the Ozarks are the most haunted place on earth. When asked what he meant by this, he would always answer, "It's all them caves we got." It's certainly true that the Ozarks are full of caves—karst topography, as they call it. Basically, beneath our feet the rock is like Swiss cheese. There's a running theory amongst many Ozarkers I've met that so many caves allow spirits of all kinds (not just ghosts) to easily travel back-and-forth from the Otherworld into this realm. Then they wander the land looking for a place to settle down, usually somewhere quiet, usually somewhere abandoned, usually a barn.

Ozarkers have traditionally had a very interesting relationship with spirits. Many of our beliefs about the Otherworld were inherited from the mishmash of cultures that fused together in Southern Appalachia before coming with small families to the Ozark Mountains around the turn of the nineteenth century. These cultural beliefs were mostly from three large European groups: Pan-British (including Scots-Irish), Pan-Celtic (including Welsh, Cornish, Scottish, and Irish), and Pan-Germanic (including German, Scandinavian, and Central European). There was a smattering of other influences, including the Canadian French-speaking communities around Old Mines in the Missouri Ozarks, along with very early Spanish and Italian influences that stuck around in tiny communities here and there. The other large area of influence came from Indigenous groups in Southern Appalachia, namely the Muskogee Creek, Cherokee, Yuchi, and Koasati (Coushatta), as well as from enslaved West and Central African peoples. The racial and cultural history of Appalachia and the Ozarks is a very complicated one. Many of the families that came to the Ozark Mountains were of mixed ancestry, bringing with them a variety of complex religious and cultural beliefs. These beliefs and traditions continued to evolve in the isolation of the Ozarks.

Spirit-beliefs here in the mountains don't just include ghosts. Many of the inhabitants of the Otherworld are often lumped under the term spirit, including, but not limited to, ghosts, haints (malign ghosts), angels, fairies, land spirits, demons, imps, etc. Any of these could be called a spirit at some point or another, as well as an angel or even a fairy, depending on who you're talking to. Fairies and other fae beings often further get lumped into the category of Little People, although one could argue the Little People are a specific type of fairy on their own. Amongst many believers of these beings, especially healers who often work with them, they are given names that would be religiously appropriate. Spirit is often culturally associated in the Ozarks with witchcraft, familiar spirits, and necromancy, all of which are strictly forbidden. So, in cases where healers might want to disguise their practice, they often refer to certain guiding spirits or helping fairies as simply angels. Few in the community would question such piety. What then is a spirit? From an Ozark perspective, I define a spirit as: a being, a personality, an identity, who is born in or spends most of their time in, the Otherworld. A fairy is a spirit because they are born from the magic of the Otherworld. A ghost or haint is a spirit because while they were born on Earth as a human being, as a soul, they returned to where all souls go after death: the Otherworld.

The Ozark Otherworld is commonly described as another place, invisible to most human beings, that's an exact mirror of this world in every detail. That's an important bit to understand. In this tradition, the Otherworld isn't above or below us, but all around us, superimposed over our world. Traditional accounts say that every detail of this world, including trees, mountains, houses even, are present in the Otherworld in some form. Likewise, what is present in the Otherworld also appears here, although often disguised. Take, for instance, the Little People, our famous Ozark fairies. They are said to have villages inside of auspicious land features like waterfalls, natural springs, lone trees, giant forest boulders, etc. While we might see a tree, rock, or waterfall, in the Otherworld these appear as beautiful cities made from gold and precious gemstones. Understanding the positioning of the Otherworld is vital to the work of the mountain exorcist (and healers in general) because what we do on this side is also done on the other side. This belief has given birth to countless cautionary anecdotes about how to treat the land, especially auspicious or rare land features, and all the amazingly wonderful curses and maladies that can result from abusing our otherworldly neighbors.

The appearance of the Otherworld often changes based on the observer. I've heard theories that for those with a good soul, the Otherworld will be a paradise, but for those who are wicked or evil, it will become a sort of hell realm. There are other features that often tell a person they might have stepped into the Otherworld. For example, many of these stories describe the quality of the light in the Otherworld as being more beautiful or shining more brilliantly than here. Others describe the colors as being more vivid or with a shimmering quality. And for some, the Otherworld is only identifiable when an unknowing human finally sees a spirit in their true form, as with one story where a man wandered lost through the woods for days before stumbling upon a city made from diamonds whose inhabitants were beautiful, winged beings made from moonlight. That would probably tip off most people to the fact that they aren't on Earth anymore.

Because of the layered nature of these two worlds, it's often very easy for beings to pass back and forth between the thin, invisible veil that separates us from the Otherworld. The veil is a sort of permeable, energetic membrane that ensures the two worlds remain separated; otherwise, chaos would no doubt ensue. The motif of accidentally stepping through the veil into the Otherworld is featured heavily in the Ozark storytelling tradition, normally as a caution against certain dangerous activities. It's said that the spirits can travel between the worlds much easier than us humans. They are seen as being more magical because the Otherworld is a place where the springs of nature's magic are closer to the surface than here. Certain humans may be born with the sight, or second sight as it's called in the Ozarks. These individuals can sense into the Otherworld in some way (sight, sound, smell, etc.) as well as often travel there either in body (rare) or through dreams. Such gifted individuals often became local spirit hunters, wranglers, and exorcists in the old days.

I decided to ask Jim a few questions before immediately agreeing to help him with his spectral situation. His message hadn't really come as a surprise as I'd been practicing as a sort of generalist spiritual healer/exorcist/spirit wrangler/whatever else anyone needed of me for a few years already. Experience and several amazing teachers over the years had taught me to gather more information before just jumping into any situation where a spirit might be involved.

ME: Sorry to hear that, what's been going on?
JIM: A HAUNTING
ME: Right, what's been happening though?
JIM: HAUNTED BARN
ME: Can you tell me what you've been experiencing in the barn that makes you think it's haunted?
JIM: WEIRD STUFF
ME: Like what?
JIM: SCRATCHING SOUNDS, MARKS ON WOOD, ALL THE TIME...AND BLOOD
ME: Blood?
JIM: YES ITS BAD CAN YOU HELP
ME: When did all this start?
JIM: 1983
ME: Oh ok so this has been happening for a while?
JIM: ALL THE TIME

Identifying spirits in Ozark folk magic takes many forms. As with most traditional practices, it seems like every healer or person with the second sight has their own unique methods. For most, divination systems play a crucial role in getting a final answer on what type of entity you're dealing with. Tarot and playing cards are common for this, as well as Ouija boards, pendulums, and the always popular dowsing rods. Dowsing seems to be used by many of the older healers and demon hunters I've worked with, as many other divinatory methods have traditionally been seen as taboo because of their association with witchcraft (fortune telling). Ozarkers have a complicated hierarchy of what does and doesn't constitute forbidden witchcraft and the list often changes depending upon the practitioner, situation, and even day of the week.

Despite the actual method used, the process is generally the same. Questions will be asked about the entity, and answers will be produced by the divinatory method. For some, this will take place at the haunted site itself, as in the case of using dowsing rods to locate a spirit within a home or using a Ouija board to communicate with the entity. Again, methodology is left up to the practitioner and their lineage of traditions. My personal techniques come from one teacher in particular. We'll talk a little bit more about her unique approach to the Otherworld and its inhabitants a little later. She always warned me against going into any spirit situation blind and taught me that any methods of diagnosis or identification should be done before arriving at the haunted site. She preferred pendulum work with simple "yes" and "no" answers, as well as information gained through dreams. In my own work, I prefer to use geomancy as my divination method when investigating spirits, but I do still utilize other traditional practices I've been taught.

Many other exorcists and practitioners leave out divinatory diagnosis altogether and prefer instead compiling "symptoms" of the haunting in order to identify what sort of spirit might be present. Here are some common symptoms I've collected. Note, these symptoms can be present both inside a building/dwelling or on the land itself and hauntings can include several spirits, resulting in a combination of symptoms:

Haints: noisy behavior; wall rapping; disembodied voices; objects moving; cabinet doors left open; doors creaking on their own; generally annoying antics.

Fairies/Little People: trickery present; objects and items in the house randomly disappearing; sudden illnesses without apparent cause; strange dreams; bad luck; money seems to disappear into thin air; fairy activity is defined by its suddenness and unusualness.

Demons: troubling or nightmarish illusions; severe illnesses or illnesses that get worse and worse; a general feeling of heat and "boiling anger"; worsening tempers; smelling sulfur/brimstone;

severe and sudden hopelessness; symptoms that disappear when not inside the home or on the land.

Witches: general "wasting" away; constant tiredness and depression; paling skin; scratching sounds, particularly in the middle of the night around anyone sleeping; strange animals seen on land or around the house; the presence of owls around the house; waking up out of breath; waking up with strange scratches on the skin.

Land Spirits: symptoms based mostly outside the home on the land; sudden insect invasions; random land effects like tree branches falling, landslides, sudden fires, unusual floods, and droughts; failing crops; lack of animal (especially bird) activity on the land.

Of course, many of these symptoms are connected to actual illnesses, and in all cases where health is being affected, I recommend immediate medical care. The cure for the haunting is almost always catered to which specific spirit is present. While there are general exorcisms as part of the Ozark folk magic repertoire, my teacher obsessively reiterated to me that hauntings are like illnesses where an over-the-counter medicine might work, but a specific cure for a specific ailment is always better.

ME: Jim are you okay with me asking some questions to make sure I know what I'm dealing with?
JIM: YES IM READY
ME: Is the blood actually there or do you just see it like a mirage?
JIM: ITS ON THE WOOD YOU CAN HEAR THE SCRATCHING
ME: Is the blood wet?
JIM: DRY
ME: When do you hear/see the scratching and blood?
JIM: NIGHT FULL MOON IS WORSE
ME: Every night?

JIM: DONT KNOW
ME: Has anyone in the family died on the land?
JIM: NO
ME: Did you build the barn?
JIM: WAS THERE WHEN I BOUGHT PROPERTY
ME: Since 1983 have you done any construction or big projects on the land?
JIM: ADDED TO THE HOUSE TEN YEARS AGO
ME: Anything on the land itself? Moved any boulders? Cut down any trees?
JIM: NO I KNOW BETTER
ME: That's good to hear

This is part of my standard list of questions when investigating a haunting. In Ozark daemonology, both the symptom of the haunting and the cure are often derived from interactions with the spirits themselves. Knowing more about these interactions can be a significant aid in developing a remedy. For example, in Jim's case, here is what certain symptoms might have told me about his specific situation:

Having illusory blood and spectral sounds can lend itself toward the activity of a haint. Haints are said to only have enough spiritual energy to manifest minor images and sounds. What manifests, while shocking, lacks a physical nature like a mirage. The energy of the haint can extend to the manipulation of objects, but a physical object is needed. They can't create new matter, nor can they even rearrange matter to form new things, as with the case of fairies, demons, and the occasional witch. The presence of real scratch marks and dried blood in Jim's barn indicated to me that this wasn't likely a haint.

The timing of the manifestations can narrow down the window of influence so as to add an identifier to the spirit. For example, manifestations that occur on days like Halloween and Christmas Eve are associated specifically with haints and other spirits of the dead in the Ozarks. They can occur on days associated with fairies, like May Eve, solstices, and equinoxes, or specific days of the week like Tuesday and Friday, both associated with demons and witches. While in the Otherworld, spirits hold an unlimited amount of power, in the mortal realm, they wax and wane with the Moon. Spirits of all kinds, but specifically haints, land spirits, and witches, are said to be at their most powerful on the full moon and weakest on the new moon. The Little People and many other fae beings, however, are said to be able to bend these rules with their magical powers and aren't often so vitally connected to the lunar cycles.

Death on the land can indicate the presence of a wandering or confused ghost-turned-haint, especially if the death occurred inside the barn itself. I've encountered this on numerous occasions, as with one case where haybales were being moved around a barn in the night, much to the annoyance of the farmer who called me. In researching the farm, it came out that the former owner had died of a heart attack while working in the barn. Even in his spirit-life, he wished to continue his chores. In cases of recent hauntings, the cause could be unknowingly guiding an errant haint back home with you from a graveyard, especially after funerals. Ozarkers traditionally have been very cautious about funerals and visiting graveyards in general and there are a variety of cleansing methods aimed at quickly detaching any haints from a person before entering back into the home. One method includes a quick wash or wipe-down with water infused with horsemint leaves (one of several varieties of the *Mondarda genus*). As Jim's haunting had continued since 1983 (and likely before he bought the property), it would be difficult to pinpoint a specific haint as the culprit, but I did some research anyway as part of my investigation and yielded no satisfying results. There disappointingly wasn't even an old family cemetery on the land, unusual for an Ozark homestead site.

Anything built on the land or any large construction projects could indicate possible negative interactions with the Little People or land spirits. Because the Ozark Mountains are such a rough landscape, human/fairy interactions have been high since the beginning of non-Indigenous settlement in the early 1800s. Scraping out a life in the early days literally meant carving flat areas of land to build houses, barns, and other necessities. The hillfolk families who settled in the Ozarks knew how to build with the landscape as best they could, but there was still a lot of disturbances across the region. In my investigations, I'd say seven out of ten issues are related to negative interactions with fairies and/or the land spirits. The old taboos of, say, not cutting down old trees, not removing solitary boulders, not plugging up natural springs, or polluting waterways, just aren't on people's minds anymore, leading to a great number of magical curses. Since Jim's haunting had started before his home renovation, I didn't suspect any fairy nonsense. It also reassured me that he was mindful of how to treat the land, lest he offend the Little People.

My questioning was beginning to point me in a very uncomfortable direction. Let's talk about witches. I should begin by saying we need to mentally travel back in time a bit for this discussion. We aren't talking about modern witches, or even about the persecutions of herbalists and wise women of the past. In Ozark folklore, witches are seen as creatures, not as human beings. They go along with other cryptids, like the monstrous, cave-dwelling *Gowrow,* the fearsome six-legged wildcat called the *Wampus,* or even fairies. Witches are sometimes also called hags, especially by German families, and there are specific types of hags that appear throughout the folklore. There's the Night Hag, who slips through an open window or a keyhole in the door and suffocates you in your sleep. Similarly, there's the Strangler, whose name is pretty self-explanatory. There's the Mule Riding Witch, who will lull a person into a deep sleep then transform them into a mule (or other mount) to ride to their diabolical sabbats. Then there are semi-helpful hags like the famed Auntie

Less, who often takes the form of an injured old woman, particularly at twilight on rural dirt roads. Those who stop to help her are rewarded with gold, gemstones, and sometimes magical powers. Those who pass by or worse, mock the poor old woman, are met with a grisly end. A similar hag is the Cooker, who appears in deep woods areas, usually cooking stew in a big cauldron outside an old, abandoned cabin. Legends say that when encountered, the Cooker will first ask if you have anything to add to the soup. This can be a scrap of food, candy, splash of water, or even seemingly inedible items, as in the case of one tale where a heartbroken woman added her lost love's scarf. Regardless, a sacrifice must be made. After adding to the soup, the Cooker will give the person a taste, thereby bestowing upon them long life and many riches. Those who refuse the Cooker are themselves added to the soup.

In Ozark folk belief, a person cannot become a witch, they can only be aligned with or in service to a witch. Many of the old timers I've talked to have been very confused about modern reimagining and reclaiming of the word "witch." For one thing, the witch is always associated with malign work in Ozark folk belief. As one storyteller told me, "If you're healing people, then you're a healer!" in response to me describing the work of modern self-proclaimed witches.

It's commonly held that certain people are born with what's called the gift. This is a divine power that is bestowed upon certain individuals who are destined to become healers. But the gift begins as a neutral power, like the magic that flows through nature itself. It's how the gifted individual chooses to use the power that determines their calling. Healers and those in service to witches are therefore seen as possessing the same divine power, but who use this gift in very different ways. As the saying goes, "Healers always heal, and witches always hurt." If the work of the gifted individual is for the growth, healing, or betterment of the individual and community at large, they are called a healer. If their work aims at harming, stealing from, scaring, or generally being a malicious nuisance to the community, they are called a witch or someone aligned with a witch. The healer is in a direct partnership with the origin of the gift itself, God. It's believed that the witch, however gifted, must work alongside a hag or other witch in order to use the neutral gift of magic in the world.

I've encountered these spectral, storybook, fairytale, or cosmic witches, as I like to call them, on a few occasions in my investigations. They're a real pain in the ass. For one thing, as a being who is more cognizant of their surroundings (unlike confused or wandering haints), they can mimic the symptoms of other hauntings, and often do, in order to trick the inhabitant or the spirit hunter. As powerful magical beings themselves, they are also dangerous when confronted and can lead to some nasty cursed conditions. They also often hold other spirits, in particular the Little People and other fairies, under their control. All these factors can ball up into a very complicated and hazardous situation indeed. My hope at the time was that it wasn't, in fact, a cosmic witch, and maybe was just some annoying fairy playing a trick. I was wrong.

Even though Jim lived a couple hours from me, the troubling symptoms he'd recounted made me nervous about the whole situation, so I agreed to try for him. That's an important phrase for traditional Ozark healers and exorcists, trying. We never say we're certain or can do anything. Ultimately, the outcome of whatever work we might be trying to do is out of our hands. It was a nice autumnal day, sunny and slightly warm for October. I packed up my exorcism kit into the car, specially curated to dealing with hags, along with a few items I also knew would be useful against fairies. Always come prepared, I heard one of my teachers whisper in the back of my mind.

Kit Contents

- 1 gallon, plastic bag of red cedar foliage
- Bible (NRSV translation)

- 3 small glass jars of sulfur powder, graveyard dirt, and camphor resin
- Leather pouch of shredded tobacco leaves
- Ceremonial wooden knife
- Ceremonial wooden cross
- 60 feet of mixed red, white, and blue paracord
- *Kangling* (Tibetan thighbone trumpet)
- Catholic rosary
- Buddhist rosary
- 1 bottle, holy water
- 1 bottle, holy oil
- Matches and a lighter
- Old cast-iron frying pan
- Oven glove with the embroidered goose wearing a blue bonnet
- Snacks (granola bars)
- Allergy meds (for the old barn)

My kit was pretty Ozark-standard, with a few noticeable exceptions that come from my Buddhist training with the spirit world. One of my most beloved teachers was a famous exorcist and medium in her part of the Ozarks. Over the years, I've collected a stack of traditional verbal charms, prayers, and rituals meant to deal with a whole host of otherworldly intruders. It seems like every Ozark healer I've met has had at least one verse of banishment. Traditionally, gifted folks wouldn't have separated physical illnesses and magical curses. They were both detected using the same diagnosis methods and addressed with the same ritual and herbal prescriptions. We're the weird ones who think there's somehow a deep divide between our bodies and souls. For this reason, it was once common for healers to have a few exorcists available to them, just in case that's where the diagnosis was pointing. In much more dire circumstances, an expert like my teacher would be called in to assist. In the past, these mountain wizards went by specific titles like Power Doctor, Goomer Doctor, Witch Master, or Witcher (no, the popular video game series didn't make up the name on their own). The word "goomer" is a curious one with unknown origins. My own opinion is that it's likely of West or Central African origin, as it's similar to other African loanwords, like "goofer" (as in the famed magical powder, goofer dust), that made their way into the Ozarks through Black communities practicing Hoodoo, Rootwork, and Southern Conjure. Goomering is witchcraft. Therefore, to be goomered is to be cursed by a witch specifically, or to goomer someone is to cast a deadly curse yourself. A Goomer Doctor is a healer skilled in doctoring goomering, or removing curses.

My teacher never called herself a Goomer Doctor. When I asked about the subject, she just waved her hand at me and answered, "Only greedy men need a title." She performed the essential role of a Goomer Doctor, albeit in her own way. When she was a much younger exorcist, she had an encounter with a ghost that forever left her and her practice changed. "I used to do all sorts of harm to spirits," she'd say, recounting the story for me. By "harm," she meant the more traditional methods of exorcism which are often very violent or at least employ violent imagery as part of the ritual process. As in one rite I collected where the exorcist holds a red cedar branch (*Juniperus virginiana*) in their right hand and visualizes chopping the spirit apart limb-from-limb along with a verbal charm with phrases like, "Spirit! Foul wanderer! I cut your legs so you can't walk! I cut your arms so you can't grab...I stab your eyes so you can't see...your ears so you can't hear..." and so on until literally every imagined part of the spirits body is severed and tossed into the Otherworld. My teacher was performing a similar ritual after having magically chained the spirit to a rock at the haunted location.

"I was wailing and chopping and cutting in a frenzy," my teacher continued with her story, "I was so fired up I didn't know where I was. Then I heard the spirit wailing something terrible. It was crying and crying. It was in pain."

In that moment, due to her own ability to see spirits, she had an awakening to the suffering she was causing another sentient being. "With my own eyes I saw her on the ground, whipped black and blue, chained to the rock. I saw her so weak and feeble she couldn't even pick up her head from off the rock...I knew I'd done something horrible."

My teacher ended up falling to the ground in tears as well. The weight of all the exorcisms she'd done fell onto her shoulders and as she wept, she heard the voice of Jesus calling to her with similar words to those he used to transform Paul on the road to Damascus, "...he said to me...'Why do you persecute me and my children?' and I didn't have an answer...and I felt him there for a long while before I came to my senses again."

After this encounter, my teacher began to develop her own tradition of Ozark spirit-work, which she called a kinder exorcism. To condense such an amazing story into a few lines, she started reading more literature from the Spiritualists and Spiritists. She was a particular fan of French founder of Spiritism, Allan Kardec, which is where she got the blueprint for her own vision of the Spiritual Hierarchy, as well as much more therapeutic approaches to spirit-interactions that were popular (and still are) amongst Spiritist groups. These are the methods that I've inherited in my own practice. While they aren't always as satisfying as the hack-and-slash sort of exorcisms, in my opinion they make for a much more meaningful interaction with our fellow sentient beings from beyond the veil.

Spiritism, as it was established by Frenchman Allan Kardec (born Hippolyte Léon Denizard Rivail), sought a more scientific approach to otherworldly phenomena. Kardec viewed the old forms of exorcism to be outdated, filled with useless pageantry, and, above all else, cruel. Kardec's Spiritism is based on the view that all beings have souls and that all these souls, no matter how ignorant, mischievous, or wise, are on the same upward progression toward union with the Divine. Traditional exorcism is then seen as harming another being, as is reflected in my teacher's conversion story. Spiritism does recognize the fact that there are entities who we might not want lurking around our homes or constantly looking over our shoulder. The methods used in traditional Spiritism are geared more toward counseling the spirit—aiding them on their own spiritual progression towards God. This is achieved in several ways, all of which utilize the power of the spirit medium to open up a line of communication with whatever entity is present. The most common method aims at getting the spirit to recognize the truth behind the ascent of souls in hopes that this will trigger reform in the naughty ones and illumination in spirits who are confused.

When I first started studying the art of the kinder exorcism, I asked my teacher what her most used method for spirit removal (or reformation) was, and she replied, "I give them the listening ear they've never had." A simple method, which fits perfectly alongside other Ozark healers who choose methods of counseling over complicated ritual. Underneath the simple surface, however, this was a profoundly complex viewpoint. Was she really saying that even demons needed some therapy every now and then? Yes, she was. Her view was often at odds with the local community, still entrenched in old views of spiritual entities and the need for hack-and-slash and kick-em-to-the-curb methods of exorcism. In one anecdote she shared with me, she had an argument with a local preacher after church one Sunday. In a big show of machismo for his gathered congregation, he laughed at her and said, "I bet you think the Devil himself can be reformed!" My teacher, who never joked with matters of spirit, replied calmly, "No one is beyond Christ's loving grace." The preacher never brought up the matter again.

Jim lived on a beautiful farm situated in the bottom of a wide valley. He'd bought the land back in the 80s, but the farm had stood there since the 1880s. The house was more-or-less new, with some original parts still featured proudly, like the old kitchen and one bedroom. The outbuildings had all been replaced over the years with the exception of the giant beast of a barn that cast a long shadow across the grassy field, left fallow. The wood was grayed and stained in places from rusty water that would pour down off the tin roof when it rained. Two open hay-windows at the roof's peak and a wide sliding door down at the ground gave the appearance of a wailing spectral face. Even the architecture was crying out for help.

As I parked my car, an old hound dog sauntered over to investigate me. He sniffed at my bag, then returned to his woolen rug on the front porch. Jim met me with a wide smile and firm handshake. He wore a blue and green flannel shirt and an old tan cowboy hat with a hawk feather stuck in the leather brim. His white mustache was waxed into curls at the tips that twitched against his cheek as he smiled. "Found the place alright?" he asked, leading me into the house.

"Yep, the GPS didn't do me wrong," I laughed.

Jim stopped on the porch and looked out toward the old barn, "Well she must not have interfered then," he said, nodding.

I paused and glanced with him out across the field. A chill went up my spine and the old hound dog grumbled at my feet. Jim slapped my shoulder, "C'mon in, coffee's on," he said, showing me inside the house.

We sat at the large, wooden kitchen table and nibbled on homemade cinnamon rolls. I got to know a bit more about Jim, which is always useful in an investigation like this. Knowing, for instance, how likely a person is to have experiences with (or even notice) spirits and otherworldly entities. Is it someone who always seems to be spinning yarns about hauntings? Or is it someone who doesn't believe in all that superstitious nonsense? Or is it even someone who might have the second sight themselves? All this information helps me not only determine how to address the spirit themselves, but also how to advise the human(s) involved. Jim was somewhere in between all these places. He was born on an auspicious day, Christmas Eve. A classic sign or token in the Ozarks that he was born with the gift. He was a level-headed guy, as far as I could tell. He expressed interest in solving the problem but admitted that he was so familiar with the haunting that it was almost a part of the farm now. I asked if he really wanted the spirit gone, and he paused, lost in thought. "I just want it happy," he answered, eyes beginning to well up.

I learned more about his interactions with the spirit. About ten years before, his wife of forty years passed away suddenly. The shock sent him into a downward spiral that, fortunately, he was able to escape from with the help of his local community and other family members. Help also came from an unlikely source—his hag-infested barn. Jim revealed another symptom of the haunting, which at the time I'd wished he'd let me know about sooner. "The thing out in the barn cries sometimes," he said nonchalantly. "After my wife passed, I'd go out and cry with it. It always helped me."

I had a million follow-up questions but quickly realized that Jim's "friendship" (if I can call it that?) with the hag was something powerful for him that I really didn't want to explain away with my analysis. Oftentimes mysteries are best left as a mystery, in my experience. It was clear through our conversation that Jim was okay with the presence in his barn but, like his kind friends who checked in on him in his time of need, he wanted to extend the same kindness to whatever spirit was present. The way he happily talked about his experiences with the various barn-phenomena didn't read to me like someone scared of what was going on. It reminded me of my own teacher as she lovingly told stories of spirits she saved and cried alongside tales of broken hearts and beloved ones gone too soon.

I'll admit, in my line of work I don't often encounter people looking at spirits like this. Most of the time, there's a lot of fear and confusion that I have to try and sort through before I even begin to deal with the spirit themselves. But it's all a part of the work! As my teacher taught me, spirits often feed off the emotions of the place they're haunting. A trickster becomes trickier the more they're noticed and the more attention they receive, very much like a toddler in that way. A run-of-the-mill noisy haint can easily become a door-slamming, plate-shattering poltergeist if given enough attention for a long enough time. Likewise, I've found that even more difficult hauntings can be solved when the human inhabitants of the space calm their own emotions first.

After breakfast, I walked Jim through my normal investigation process. I always begin with just walking through the space and seeing what my gut is telling me. Then I normally do a geomancy reading, which paints a detailed portrait of the energies flowing through the area and offers some sense of what form the spirit is taking. From there, I develop a plan of action. Sometimes that involves immediate work, like smoke or water cleansing in the space. In cases where a spirit might need to be overpowered, I will wait for an auspicious day to roll around, like the new moon, for example. Ozark folk magic in general, and spirit work specifically, is all based in processes of diagnosis and treatment. There are no one-shot cures in Ozark folk magic. Even things like cleansing, which will clear the energies of the space, are still followed with additional diagnosis, usually using divination or dreams. I told Jim that I might need to return to do additional work, depending on the reading, and he happily agreed. "Just good to know there's youngsters still doing this," he said with a smile.

We headed toward the barn. The old hound dog started to follow us, but seeing the direction we were taking, he returned back to his spot. That made me nervous at first, but Jim just laughed and said, "Don't worry, he's scared of his own shadow."

The old barn was, well, an old barn. The wide, sliding door creaked loudly as I helped Jim open up the entrance. Sunlight poured into the space, causing angular shadows to retreat away into their corners. The floor was covered in a thin layer of old hay. A few pieces of large farm equipment sat silent and motionless around the periphery, covered in dust and moldy canvas tarps. Jim led me over to one of the nine large wooden posts that connected the floor to the hay loft above us. "Here it is," Jim said, pointing up toward the top of one of the posts.

A sunbeam from a hole in the roof lit up the old, graying wood marked with termite holes and mildew. Red streaks ran down the post, beginning where it met the ceiling then down about three feet. It looked like it continued around the entire circumference of the post. The red liquid shimmered in the sunlight but remained otherwise motionless, frozen in place like hardened resin. "Has it grown or diminished in size ever?" I asked, staring up toward the ceiling.

"It's been that way ever since I bought the place," Jim answered.

He went on to explain that he never had a chance to look through the old barn before purchasing the land, as it had been crammed full of broken equipment and a lifetime's worth of junk. "Bought it on sight," he laughed. "Probably should have looked around more."

Jim took out a small flashlight from his coat pocket and shined a light further down on the post where the sunbeam hadn't landed. There were long, deep gouges in the wood like some massive cat had used it to sharpen its claws. "And this is where you hear the scratching?" I asked, running my fingertips through the gouges.

Jim nodded, "But they don't change. I just hear the scratching. It's loudest on the full moon, but you can hear it now and then. Always at night, and sometimes with the wailing."

I was lost in my thoughts. This often happens in new spaces, where my own spirit will be led through the emotions and energies of the place. The air felt cold and heavy, despite the warmth of the day outside. A gloom hung in the space like a spectral fog. Even the few beams of sunlight piercing in through the roof seemed to bend and try to retreat away from the darkness below. It wasn't a feeling of evil, I always hesitate to use that word, it was just a feeling of sadness and heaviness. I was brought back to the space by Jim's hand on my shoulder, "I'll leave you to it," he said quietly. I nodded then returned to pondering.

I fear this tale of intrigue and horror might end as a bit of a disappointment to some of you. My intention in spinning this yarn is to give a good glimpse into the processes behind my work as an Ozark daemonologist and spirit hunter. The reality of this work is that it involves a whole lot of pondering, talking, and processing energies. You'll find this with a lot of things in the Ozark Mountains—the stories are often far stranger than the reality. When I was working with my teacher for the kinder exorcism, I was sadly under the impression that I was going to see things that shocked and amazed me. While I did see a lot of amazing things, it was never the spirit battles and eldritch confrontations of legends and movies. What I saw were families healed, emotions settled, old memories recounted, and feuds forgiven. Interactions with spirits often brings out what has been buried, hidden, and left for dead. In my experience, hauntings teach us less about the spirit that is present and more about how we're feeling and reacting in a specific situation. In healing the ghosts and devils around us, in working through unraveling these countless knots of pain and strife, we often somehow manage to work through our own demons as well.

I ended up doing three separate geomancy readings for Jim's haunted barn. Each result was nearly the same portrait of the space. Grief. Loss. Mourning. But the last reading, which came after I did a traditional red cedar smoke cleanse of the energies, revealed an unexpected additional emotion—hope. The mysterious thing in the barn, whatever it was, was processing its own trauma. As I packed up my notepad and tools back into my exorcism bag, I caught a brief sensorial glimpse, a mental image not of my own that flashed like steel striking against flint before disappearing again. Jim's presence, his love and care for whatever was there in the barn, his love and care for the land, his own experience of grief and coming to terms with the great loss he'd experienced, all of it was helping this spirit to heal as well. We always forget how connected we can be to the spirits around us. Our own souls, spirits embodied in flesh, reach out to our unseen siblings in times of great strife and need. As we heal, they heal.

I gave my full report to Jim later that day over a cup of coffee at his dining room table. I asked if he had any notion about what I was going to tell him and he smiled and nodded. He told me he'd had a dream the night before, the first one he'd ever had of the spirit in the barn. He was crying at his wife's grave when he felt a warm hand on his shoulder. He turned, thinking it was his wife returned, but there instead stood a strange old woman in a patchwork dress, heart and hands covered in blood. Jim said he wasn't scared, although he knew he probably should be. He stood and wiped the woman's tears away and said, "We'll get through it, don't worry." The old woman smiled and fell forward into Jim's open arms.

"What do you think the dream means for you?" I asked, my heart overjoyed for this resolution.

Jim smiled and wiped some tears from his eyes with his gnarled, calloused hands, "Well, I reckon it means we'll get through this."

I agreed. I left Jim with my professional opinion, "Don't be afraid, and pray for her, whoever she is." He nodded and showed me to my car. On my way back home, I processed what I'd learned through this experience. Every case is different. It's almost as if spirits are sentient beings with their own emotions, thoughts, experiences, motivations, etc. Who would have thought? I never leave an investigation the same, there's always something to be gained, no matter what happens. On this occasion, I was reaffirmed in my belief that even the strangest of phenomena—blood, scratches, wailing—can be masking a very relatable state of grief and sorrow. By lending a listening ear, as my teacher taught me, we can relate to the spirits around us not as master and mastered, but as fellow wanderers through the universe who sometimes need help.

Brujería Mexicana

by Laura Davila

Writing a contribution for an anthology about the magical systems and practices of the world—particularly my section on Mexican Brujería—is a serious responsibility. Even after writing two books, participating in podcasts, blogs, symposiums, and teaching classes, I didn't fully realize until today how difficult it would be to do justice to this practice in only a few thousand words. The word *Brujería* itself means different things to different people. It is a broad and complex term used by millions across the Spanish-speaking world, and it extends far beyond Mexico or Latin America.

In contemporary Mexico, *bruja, brujo,* or *bruje* can refer to anyone who practices any form of magic—spells, herbalism, divination, astrology, folk religion, or ritual work. To speak of Brujería Mexicana requires placing the practice within its long timeline, its rich history, and its deep connection to territory. My goal is to introduce the reader to the two most conventional styles of Brujería that come to mind for most Mexicans when we hear the words "Brujería Mexicana."

To begin a discussion about a practice rooted in the syncretism of Mexican culture, I want to paraphrase Mexican writer, diplomat, and philosopher Alfonso Reyes, who described Mexican identity—what he called *mexicanidad*—in a way that also describes our magical traditions. He wrote that from the fragile terracotta vessel lovingly molded by hand to the iron forged under relentless hammer blows, it is natural that from the union of such different characters an entirely new product emerges, yet one in which both origins can still be recognized, sometimes alternating, sometimes interwoven in paradox.

This hybrid identity is visible everywhere in contemporary Mexico—not only in our people, but in our food, art, celebrations, and especially our magical traditions. The traits of the old world and the new world, of the conquered and the conquerors, remain intertwined.

Brujería Mexicana is an ancient and ever-evolving practice. It combines pre-Hispanic and colonial beliefs, Mexican folk Catholicism, animism, political realities, and centuries of oral traditions preserved through legends and folktales. It is a living system that has absorbed influences from around the world and continues to grow.

For the average Mexican, la brujería is a way of weaving together the sacred and the profane when facing adversity, fear, or despair. It is a way to call upon magical allies: pre-Hispanic deities, enduring mystics, Catholic saints, and folk saints born from our wounded and resilient Mexico, such as Santa Muerte, Jesús Malverde, or Juan Soldado.

Brujería Mexicana and its practitioners are not a monolith. They are shaped by regional differences, historical periods, personal ethics, local customs, social conditions, and the sociotechnical realities of each generation. To claim that there is only one "traditional" way to practice Brujería would erase important groups, time periods, and traditions that contributed to the way the craft is practiced today. Understanding this requires taking seriously the cultural, mystical, and folkloric syncretism that has been simmering for nearly six centuries.

Cultural Brujería in Mexico

Unlike many esoteric or initiatory traditions around the world, Brujería in Mexico is deeply embedded in our cultural heritage. This is why most Mexicans, whether they claim the title witch or not, have at least some background in Brujería. We grow up surrounded by practical rites and everyday rituals from dawn to dusk.

There is a common belief in Mexico that magical knowledge is passed down through our elders, especially the women of previous generations. Grandmothers in particular have acted as guardians of customary prayers, herbal remedies, healing techniques, everyday rituals, and folk Catholic devotions. This oral tradition ensures that Brujería remains accessible regardless of social class or economic resources.

Everyone with the right mindset can practice cultural Brujería. It doesn't require initiation, baptism, or formal esoteric education. Many people even refer to folk Catholicism itself as a form of cultural Mexican Brujería. The tools of the practice—herbs, candles, water, salt, images of saints, alcohol, eggs, mirrors, brooms, fruits, and kitchen staples—are usually already present in any Mexican household.

Cultural brujas and brujos tend to be eclectic and autodidactic. They learn through personal experience, through sharing knowledge with other practitioners, through books, or even through modern technology—online classes, mentorships, and digital communities.

This is not an institutionally recognized practice. It is an everyday occurrence, driven by need, intuition, and faith. The goals of cultural Brujería are not categorized as "good" or "bad," but rather as attempts to restore balance, respond to injustice, or address the absence of solutions in official institutions. Brujería becomes rebellion, survival, protection, and a spiritual method of dealing with inequity, impunity, or despair.

Cultural Brujería is guided by the practitioner's own moral compass—their sense of right and wrong, shaped by their community, their experiences, and their personal ethics. Most importantly, it is not a closed practice. People from other cultures may explore it respectfully, just as one would be welcomed into a Mexican household when entering with humility and care. Many of our folk saints, including Santa Muerte, are open to anyone who seeks them sincerely.

Sources That Feed Brujería Mexicana

Our earliest ancestors were deeply animistic. Most native tribes that now form the territory we call Mexico believed that everything in the world possessed a spirit. Hundreds of these spirits were petitioned for rain, healing, protection, or the reversal of misfortune. Some spirits were called upon to cure, others to harm.

This worldview still echoes in our practices today, though often hidden beneath Catholic language. Illness, misfortune, and bad luck may still be explained as effects of envy, spiritual interference, or intentional harm sent consciously or unconsciously by another person. Although the names of spirits have changed, the beliefs themselves endure.

Mexico is the second-largest Catholic nation in the world, with more than 97 million Catholics according to the 2020 census. Many of the rituals associated with the Virgin Mary—especially the devotion to Our Lady of Guadalupe—alongside prayers, saintly intercessions, novenas, and Catholic invocations, have become deeply integrated into Brujería Mexicana.

Spirits in the practice can be broadly understood in classes. There is a supreme Creator spirit, and from this Creator all other spirits emerged, each with different roles and missions. It is accepted in Mexican Brujería that both benevolent and malevolent spirits exist, and that they oppose each other while still fulfilling the purposes they were created for.

Even in pre-Hispanic times, magic and religion were inseparable. Consider Tezcatlipoca and Quetzalcóatl—one tasked with creating, the other with destroying. Today these cosmic laws are translated into Dios Padre (God the Father), San Miguel Arcángel, Lucifer, the Devil, and other spiritual forces. The names changed, but the structure remained familiar.

The Mexican Brujería Triad: Dios, el Diablo, and La Muerte

The iconic triad—God, the Devil, and Death—is a powerful emblem of Mexican spirituality. It appears in our art, festivals like Día de Muertos, magical systems, and collective worldview.

Mexicans live with a deep awareness of death. We celebrate it, joke about it, dance with it, fear it, and honor it. Because of this, many magical repertoires include death-related deities and folk saints such as San Pascualito (venerated in southern Mexico and Guatemala) and, of course, Santa Muerte, beloved worldwide.

Mexico exists in tension. There is light, darkness, and the vast territory in between. Political corruption, poverty, femicide, narco-violence, breathtaking landscapes, extraordinary cuisine, and immense artistic beauty coexist side by side. This paradox shapes our spirituality.

Mexican brujas walk all three paths—the right, the left, and the forward one. They petition angels, saints, shadows, and spirits with equal fluency. The triad exists because Mexico is a reflection of it.

Dios (God and Divine Providence)

For most Mexicans, whether they practice witchcraft or not, faith begins with God. God manifests in three ways: God the Father, God the Son (Jesus), and God the Holy Spirit. All three are entirely divine, yet each has distinct characteristics.

God the Father is seen as the supreme Creator, omnipotent, omniscient, omnipresent. Jesus is the incarnate Word. The Holy Spirit is the presence of God within us. Together they are the givers of divine providence—the ones who grant shelter, food, protection, and sustenance.

Images of Divine Providence are common on home altars and in the spaces of cultural practitioners. Most Mexicans believe that not even a leaf moves without the will of God.

San Miguel Arcángel

San Miguel Arcángel is both a spiritual ally and a cultural icon. He is perhaps the most beloved figure among Mexican witches. No market, herb shop, or botánica in Mexico is complete without images, perfumes, charms, statues, or amulets of Saint Michael, such as his sword, shield, or scales.

According to Catholic tradition, on April 25, 1631, the archangel appeared three times to a 17-year-old boy named Diego Lázaro in what is now Tlaxcala. He revealed a miraculous spring whose waters were said to cure illness. Today the Sanctuary of San Miguel del Milagro stands in that town.

There is neither a single elder practitioner of Brujería nor a book on Mexican Brujería that does not include spells, protections, or revocations invoking San Miguel.

Santa Muerte

If you are not a devotee and only know Santa Muerte from the media, then most of your information is incorrect. She is often misrepresented and unfairly associated with crime, narcotics, or violence. In reality, Santa Muerte is the patroness of the desperate Mexican, the guardian of the marginalized—LGBTQ communities, sex workers, women, immigrants, the poor. She is the saint who never discriminates.

Santa Muerte is depicted as a skeletal figure holding a scythe, scale, globe, rosary, rose, owl, hourglass, or staff. Her most traditional robes are white, black, and red—colors tied to her Indigenous roots. Academics and practitioners disagree about her exact origins, but most accept that she emerged from the syncretism of Mesoamerican, Mayan, and Catholic beliefs.

La Blanca (the White One)

The white aspect represents bones, structure, purity, healing, cleansing, and inner child work. Devotees call upon La Blanca for healing addictions, clearing blockages, and restoring mental health.

La Negra (the Black Robe)

The black aspect represents shadow work, necromancy, domination, and the left-hand path of Mexican spirituality. She is considered the favorite among many brujas for witchcraft.

La Roja (the Red Robe)

The red aspect represents blood, passion, sex, anger, romance, and emotional intensity. She is invoked for love spells, reconciliations, lust, and matters of the heart.

The modern growth of Santa Muerte devotion began in 2001 when Enriqueta Romero, affectionately known as Doña Queta, placed a shrine to Santa Muerte outside her home in Tepito. She became the guardian of the Tepito Santa Muerte and an important figure in the spread of the devotion."

Another influential leader was Enriqueta Vargas, known as La Madrina, who presided over the International Temple of Santa Muerte. She inherited leadership after the violent death of her son, Jonathan Legaria Vargas, known as El Comandante Pantera.

Neither Doña Enriqueta Romero nor Enriqueta Vargas identified as witches. Doña Queta Romero has famously said with her sharp Tepito humor: "*No doy limpias, no amarro pendejos, no leo cartas, no hago nada.*"

For her, devotion to Santa Muerte is a matter of faith, not witchcraft.

Today Santa Muerte is not only a folk saint but a global icon. She is especially revered by Mexican immigrants in the United States. Devotees ask her for love, marriage, healing, protection, safety, justice, and deliverance from spiritual or physical harm.

Although she is not canonized by the Catholic Church, most of her followers identify as Catholic or culturally Catholic. Devotion to Santa Muerte does not require exclusive worship. Many Mexicans simultaneously honor canonical saints and folk saints.

San Pascualito Rey

San Pascualito is a folk saint venerated in Guatemala and southern Mexico. He is known by many names: El Rey San Pascual, King of the Graveyard, San Pascualito Muerte, El Viejo, Rey Pascual, and more. He is associated with healing, illness, and health work. He is often depicted as a dancing skeleton wearing a cape or crown.

Like many Mexican and Guatemalan devotions, he has a syncretic background combining Catholic and Indigenous (especially Mayan) components. He is connected to San Pascual Baylón, though they are not the same spirit.

One legend says that in 1650, during an epidemic called cucumatz fever, a severely ill Indigenous man had a vision of a tall skeleton dressed in bright clothes. The figure introduced himself as San Pascual Bailón and promised to intercede if the community adopted him as their patron. He predicted that the sick man would die nine days later and that the epidemic would end. Both predictions came true. His devotion spread rapidly.

El Diablo (the Devil)

The Devil is one of the most versatile folkloric characters in Mexico. He appears in legends, in Indigenous traditions blended with Catholic beliefs, and in regional magical systems. Here are three of the most emblematic devil figures.

El Chamuco

Recognizable from Mexican lotería cards and statues, El Chamuco is a tall, red-skinned creature with horns, pointed ears, a dragon tail, and mismatched legs—one goat's leg, one crow's foot. He may carry a trident, a bottle of alcohol, or burning charcoal.

The word *chamuco* comes from *chamuscar,* meaning "to burn." He is a folkloric version of the Devil, especially in the ranching regions of northeastern Mexico. People petition the Chamuco for love, business success, protection, victory over enemies, and revenge. Though influenced by Catholic imagery of evil, El Chamuco is also humorous, familiar, and deeply rooted in popular culture.

El Angelito Negro

In Tepito, the "barrio bravo" of Mexico City, the Angelito Negro has his own chapel. He is depicted as a black angel dressed as a mariachi. Devotees leave flowers, candles, cigarettes, alcohol, toys, and money. Politicians, athletes, housewives, and even people involved in criminal groups come to him when they have nowhere else to turn.

His cult has grown nationally and internationally; there are chapels dedicated to him in San Francisco, California, and Pachuca, Hidalgo.

El Charro Negro

Readers of my book *Mexican Sorcery* will recognize El Charro Negro, a diabolic being who appears in Indigenous and rural regions across Mexico. Among the Mazatecs, he is considered either the Devil himself or the shadow of Saint Martin of Tours.

His devotees work with him only at night. Those who seek money from him must be sexually abstinent and bring offerings such as chili peppers, cacao, or a turkey. He appears as a tall, flirtatious man with a pale complexion, dressed in a black charro suit with silver spurs.

Brujería in Catemaco, Veracruz: The "Elite" Brujería

The style of Brujería most widely associated with Mexico in popular imagination is the Brujería practiced in the municipality of Catemaco, Veracruz. This tradition has diverse origins rooted in Indigenous peoples of the region, particularly the Olmecs, followed by the Mexica, Spanish colonizers, and enslaved Africans. Their combined beliefs formed what we now recognize as the Brujería of Catemaco.

The name *Catemaco* comes from Nahuatl: *calli* (houses) and *tematli* (burn), meaning "place of burned houses." The name arose after an eruption of the San Martín volcano in the Sierra de Los Tuxtlas.

Catemaco is famous for being the "land of witches." Thousands travel there yearly—everyday citizens, politicians, celebrities, and tourists—seeking healing, money, protection, love, answers, or magical remedies when nothing else has worked.

One legend says that the Virgin Mary appeared in the cave "El Tegal," near the Catemaco lagoon, to a fisherman named Juan Catemaxca in the seventeenth century. Another story says the region became magically powerful when the only white monkey in the area died, transferring its wisdom to a brujo.

But no legend is more influential than that of Gonzalo Aguirre Pech, the Brujo Mayor, who supposedly made a pact with the Devil in exchange for wisdom and magical power. He died on September 21, 1982—the same date his teacher Don Manuel Utrera died thirteen years earlier. His nine children maintain the traditions of the Tuxtlas.

The Famous Misa Negra (Black Mass)

The Misa Negra is a ceremony held in honor of the Prince of Darkness on the first Friday of March. It is considered one of the most powerful rituals in the region. Though controversial and often labeled as Satanic, the Catemaco Black Mass aims to connect with ethereal power, seek spiritual protection, renew pacts, and obtain favors from mystical entities.

The ceremony includes several acts: shedding human blood at the foot of an inverted cross; sacrificing a goat for purification; the Brujo Mayor performing the sacrifice while attendees raise their hands to receive the goat's blood; and a private ceremony in the Cueva del Diablo, accessible only by walking through dense vegetation.

Inside the Cueva del Diablo, illuminated by red lights, stands an enormous statue of the Devil with a pronounced phallus. Locals consider it an entrance to hell.

Another symbolic act is the burning of the six-pointed star late at night, accompanied by the heavy scents of incense, ocote, patchouli, seven machos cologne, herbs, and mezcal.

Though genuine witches, shamans, and healers still work in the Tuxtlas, seekers must be cautious. Catemaco has become a target for scammers exploiting vulnerable people. This is one reason cultural Brujería throughout Mexico continues to strengthen—people are reclaiming their own magic instead of outsourcing it. Others seek traditional elite Brujería in places like La Petaca (Nuevo León), Naica (Chihuahua), or Santa María de los Ángeles (Aguascalientes).

What remains constant is that Mexicans have enormous faith in the intangible. Witchcraft, magic, and the rituals of our people persist because, despite changing times, we still face many of the same sociocultural challenges of the past.

Bibliography

Dávila, Laura. *Mexican Sorcery: A Practical Guide to Brujería de Rancho*, Weiser Books, 2023.

—. *Mexican Magic: Brujería, Spells, and Rituals for All Occasions*, Weiser Books, 2024.

Coltman, Jeremy D. and John M. D. Pohl. *Sorcery in Mesoamerica*, University Press of Colorado, 2021.

De la Serna, Jacinto. *Manual de Ministros de Indios para el Conocimiento de sus Idolatrías y Extirpación de Ellas*, Imprenta del Museo Nacional, 1656.

González Soriano, Enrique; Dirzo, Rodolfo; and C. Richard. *Historia Natural de los Tuxtlas.*

Olmos, José. *Santos Populares: La Fe en Tiempos de Crisis*, Penguin Random House Grupo Editorial, 2016.

Hacks, Héctor. *Libro Negro: Tratado de Ciencias Ocultas*, Edicomunicación S.A., 1992.

Illes, Judika. *Encyclopedia of Mystics, Saints, and Sages*, HarperOne, 2011.

In Between Two Altars

Italian-American Folk Magic & Dual Faith Perspectives

by Frankie Castanea

The first time I heard about Saint magic, it was conspicuously Catholic. My mother was talking about my Nana, "When Nana did her novena, it was magic. It made things happen."

Nana was, in all senses of the word, a good Catholic. She went to church. She prayed her rosary. In my eyes, there was only Christianity and not much else, and in my nana's case, that may have been true. Later, when I finally performed her novena, Our Lady of the Miraculous Medal fulfilled my request within three days.

Understanding how a self-proclaimed witch and folk practitioner can not only pray to the Saints, but receive a response is a highly contested topic. Many traditional Catholics consider this kind of interaction and relationship to be disrespectful, and many pagans consider a proximity to Christianity as being a Christian and supporting the Church. The concept of dual faith, by itself, is one that is only beginning to be explored in the online witchcraft and occult community with different responses.

Dual faith, as we will explore, is a concept that many folk practitioners are aware of, even if they don't have the words to describe it. Dual faith is to petition Saints in one breath but dance with the Devil at the crossroads in another. It is to utilize psalms from the Bible but do magical workings the average Christian would gawk at. It is the capability to recognize the duality that exists within folk magic and culture. It is to exist between two altars—one for your patron Saint, and one for an ancient pagan goddess. To understand this, we have to dive deeper.

Italy's history is rarely as simple as it seems. Throughout the decades, different groups have placed their influences within the very small country, which wasn't always a country. To understand Italian-American folk magic's relationship with Saints, we have to understand a few elements of cultural context from Italy itself.

Italy was unified in 1861, with a movement called Il Risorgimento. Before this, Italy was not Italy, but the Kingdom of Two Sicilies, the Papal States, and many small regions that had their own languages, ways of living, and communities. These languages are not always recognized, yet they are spoken by living members of the region. Sicilian, Neapolitan, Calabrese, Piedmontese, Sardinian, and more exist across what is now the country of Italy. Many different forces have occupied or had control over what we understand to be "Italy"—the Roman Empire, Greece, Spain, the Phoenicians, and many others. Each gave its influence to the region it occupied.

While they're not all are colonizing forces, we can see some remnants of the beliefs they held in Italian culture. The very common Italian playing cards, used to play briscola, scopa, and numerous other games, have more Spanish artistic influence in the South and French and German artistic influence in the North. Remains of Ancient Greek temples to pagan gods still exist, some preserved, some buried, in Southern Italy. In some cases, such as La Madonna di Polsi and Madonna di Montevergine, the churches now dedicated to these apparitions of Mary are built on top of the remains of an earlier temple or were originally a space of worship for earlier gods. La Madonna della Montagna/La Madonna di Polsi was once two sanctuaries to Persephone and Aphrodite (Vaudoise), and La Madonna di Montevergine's temple stands upon the remains of a temple to Cybele. In the context of Saint magic, Italy was, in many ways, a battleground for the Catholic Church to sway then-pagans to becoming Christians, eventually leading to the syncretism of Saints and non-Christian gods. The Roman Empire is credited with pushing the force of Christianity and the denomination of Catholicism throughout a major span of regions. As this occurred, there was syncretism within Italy and its current religious structures. The Church itself was a force to be reckoned with, placing the Festival of the Assumption of Mary only mere days away from the Nemoralia, a festival to celebrate Diana, a Roman goddess of the hunt, and yet the pushback from everyday Italians against the institution was palpable.

The Church, in many ways, represented a force that was pushing to take away traditions and enforce change. Throughout folklore, we have remnants of this hesitation and pushback, specifically in folktales and persistent narratives. When I began my practice, I attempted to work with and venerate Saint Peter, yet my family had reservations. "I don't remember my family liking Saint Peter that much," my mom explained, "I don't remember why. But we didn't like him."

Later, through folktales and information from teachers, I received confirmation on why Italian-Americans may be hesitant around Saint Peter. He held the keys to Heaven which often led him to be syncretized with road-opening spirits in other traditions. Yet, he is also referred to as the rock of Christ's Church. Throughout anthropological sources and folk magic itself, we can see a pushback against what the Church represented through Italian-American folk magic—in *Italian Folk Magic: Rue's Kitchen Witchery* by Mary-Grace Fahrun, she describes a curse that utilizes bitten or torn off pieces of a lemon during a particular Midnight Mass sermon. In *Italian-American Folklore* by Frances M. Malpezzi and William M. Clements, a cure for *mal'occhio,* or the evil eye, is described, yet this same prayer was utilized to cast a curse upon a scorned lover using the Eucharist.

Folk magic, especially Italian-American folk magic, met between the sacred and the profane. Agostino Taumaturgo, in the *The Things We Do: Ways of the Holy Benedetta,* writes of *stregoneria,* the Italian word for witchcraft, "Stregonerian's generally don't claim any pseudohistory at all (or any history beyond this is what my mother taught me), and many consider themselves devout Catholics.... However, its intentions are not in accord with the Catholic Faith, and therefore any use of Catholic sacramentals is an act of sacrilege" (117). Yet throughout his book, he utilized Catholic elements to perform rituals and folk medicine that the American Catholic Church would most likely disagree with, such as the usage of divination with fava beans, exorcism not performed by a sanctified Church member, and freezing an individual that you no longer want in your life. The delineation between *stregoneria* and modern-day Italian folk magic seems to be minimal, if even existent. *Benedicaria* refers to a term given by Italian-Americans to Italian-American folk magic based in Catholicism, while *stregoneria,* having a negative connotation in the Italian language, appears to be a term that is rarely used to describe Italian folk magic and witchcraft practice. The term in itself, witch or *strega/streghe,* may change depending on region and may refer to an individual who casts workings to "take" from others, such as one who casts the *mal'occhio* intentionally or someone who works *fatture,* death invoices or curses. In many ways, Italian-American folk magic has been syncretized with and influenced by Catholicism, yet there are nuances with how Italian-Americans interact with Saints, magic, and Catholicism.

Saints as holy beings, are not just limited to Catholicism. Two kinds of Saints appear historically. These are canonized Saints, or those recognized by the Church, and folk Saints, or those recognized by the people. Both Mary-Grace Fahrun and Dee Norman, in their respective books on Italian-American folk magic, insist that one does not have to be Catholic to work with these energies and benefic figures. Many different traditions, including initiatory traditions, include Saints as entities that can be petitioned, venerated, and worked with to receive particular outcomes. One of the first books I read was *The Magical Power of Saints: Evocation and Candle Rituals* by Reverend Ray T. Malbrough, discussing different novenas, candle colors, and more that can be utilized to ask Saints for assistance in mundane and magical matters. Even if the Saints as spirits may not be called on in a tradition, statues of them may be used or they may represent "faces" for different spirits that have existed longer than Christianity.

In Italian-American folk magic, there are Saints that tend to take a more important role. La Madonna or the Virgin Mary, San Giuseppe or Saint Joseph, Saint Anthony of Padua, Saint Lucy of Syracuse, Sant'Agata or Saint Agatha are a few to be named. These Saints aren't always Italian, rather they are Saints that are important to the needs of the community in which they are petitioned. The patron Saint of Cosenza, my ancestors' hometown, is La Madonna di Pilerio, Our Lady of the Pillar—a Madonna who appeared and took the plague away from the people of Cosenza. Yet, this name is only found in a few other places—namely Spain—and the picture utilized to represent this apparition is a Byzantine relic.

Malpezzi and Clements write of the relationship of Italian-Americans to Saints:

> *When a peasant leaves his native village, he will forget everything but his patron saint. So far well and good. The trouble is that he makes all kinds of bargains with him, ranging from offering to burn a candle before the image of a saint if the latter will help him to carry out a business transaction, to promising to bring a twenty dollar bill when the statue of the saint is to be carried through the streets if he can have the honour of being one of the bearers. A good lady said in reply to my question as to whether she had gone to church on Easter, "I go to church on St Anthony's Day. He is my favorite saint and is more powerful than Christ, for he has performed more miracles than he. Besides, he is so handsome." (116).*

By their definitions and most folks' understandings, these individuals are good Catholics. It would be disrespectful in many ways to refer to them as witches or someone who is not a Catholic, because Catholicism in different cultural contexts holds a different meaning than what we understand on Turtle Island and within so-called-America to be Catholicism and Christianity. Folk practitioners, by many modern definitions, are "good Catholics" who do things the Church wouldn't agree with. They may drip oil into water to relieve the *mal'occhio.* They may call on Saints to heal certain ailments with specific secret prayers, such as in the tradition of Segnature (Puca), or in instances of healing Saint Anthony's Fire, or *fuoco di Sant'Antonio.*

As I was taught by Lisa Fazio, owner of the Root Circle and author of *Della Medicina: The Tradition of Italian-American Folk Healing,* these secret prayers often have a particular formula. They often invoke an entity or holy being in order to heal. We can only muse and theorize on who, before Catholicism, was invoked, but oftentimes we see traditions such as folk magic persist even if they syncretize and change face. Saints such as Saint John the Baptist are celebrated on specific days in Italy—La Notte di San Giovanni asks us to gather herbs and flowers to submerge in water overnight to collect his tears. This same water is then used to wash our faces and hands in the morning after. La Notte di San Giovanni takes place on the summer solstice, the longest day of the year, solidifying an association with San Giovanni and the Sun. The tradition of making *l'acqua di San Giovanni,* or St John's Water, is certainly not a Catholic tradition, but it is folk magic. The water acquires curative properties overnight by collecting the dew, and to wash your face in it is to bless yourself and others for the year to come. Some folks, as Karyn Crisis writes, use one hundred herbs in these waters while others use only what is available to them. Flowers, herbs with medicinal properties, and more are used in these waters, and the tradition is one that can only be done once a year.

In the same vein, the Epiphany is highly celebrated in Italian-American folk magic. The time between Christmas and l'Epifania is a time of portals, cleansing, and ritual. We often lean into the liminal space that this time provides. On l'Epifania, children are visited by La Befana, the Christmas witch, who my teacher Mary-Beth Bonfiglio linked to Strina, the Roman/Sabine goddess of the new year. In the book *Vestiges of Ancient Manners and Customs, Discoverable in Modern Italy and Sicily* by Reverend John J. Blunt, he writes of La Befana, "This Befana appears to be heir at law of a certain heathen goddess called Strenia, who presided over the new-year's gifts, 'Strenae,' from which, indeed, she derived her name. Her presents were of the same description as those of the Befana—figs, dates, and honey" (120). Bonfiglio also writes, "Perhaps Befana is the conductor for both these ancient goddesses—she sweeps away the old year, allowing it to die {Hecate} making room for healing and newness and good omens in the new year {Strenua}."

Throughout different cultures, and especially in my experience as an Italian-American folk practitioner, we can often see remnants of earlier traditions within still existing folk magics. While many of these traditions now have a face that is more palatable to the mainstream, such as Catholicism or Christianity, it is difficult to remove a culture, magic, or a tradition from a group of people.

From my teachers and from my own experience with the magic, I slowly learned that Saints, while they are figures that must be respected, are often faces for beings and energies that may have existed long before the Church did. While La Befana is a folkloric figure that may have changed over time, she is heavily associated with the Epiphany, a Christian holiday, and the Three Kings, Christian figures that bring presents to Jesus Christ when he is born. Other Saints may have died and been martyred as people, but are associated and drawn with certain symbolism in death that links them to other, ancient forces. Santa Rosalia is a wonderful example of this. Many of her paintings show her with a skull on top of a book or picture her holding a skull. The skull, in these drawings, is apparently hers and represents her martyrdom and life as a hermit. Yet, one can't help but notice more necromantic symbols. Her image, as my friend Gigi says, pays homage to earlier, pre-Christian funerary rites, "Rosalia was an ancient Roman festival intended to honor the dead and celebrate the beauty of life. During this festival, mourners would make flower crowns and wreathes with roses and violets. These crowns and wreaths were not only left as offerings to the dead, but were used to decorate statues of goddesses associated with the festival." While we understand Santa Rosalia as a protectress against plague, she is often linked with death, grief, and mourning due to the imagery used for her after she was canonized.

This, in many ways, tracks with my personal experiences with Saints and Gods. At the beginning of my practice, there was a hesitation with Saints. How could I work with these beings who are so against what I believe? And yet, the Saints themselves are not the Church. I do not work with the Saints because I love the institution that has contributed to various harms across continents and forced conversions of my own ancestors. In fact, when I started my practice, I didn't think I would work with Saints at all. I considered myself pagan. Despite having altars to Saints and to my ancestors, I still felt hesitant about moving towards petitioning to Saints, and I had little luck in receiving a response. Yet, as I dived deeper into ancestor work and ancestral magic, I kept trying. Eventually, we came into possession of my late grandmother's belongings, and I found two sets of prayers stapled together, the novena of Our Lady of the Miraculous Medal and the prayer to Saint Anthony of Padua. I spent time trying both prayers for various purposes. At the time, I was not a Catholic in the sense that I didn't define myself as such. I didn't work with Saints, didn't attend church, and more. I knew little to nothing about Saint magic and petitioning, but both of the Saints in my petitions answered me incredibly quickly. In many ways, this experience allowed me a deeper understanding of Saints as energetic beings and entities—many are incredibly benefic. Many, in my opinion, remember who you are and who your family is, especially if those family members had a long-standing relationship with them. As I talked to Saints, I was consistently receiving the feeling that I wasn't just talking to a Saint. It was a Saint, but in many cases, especially those of well-known Saints utilized by folk witches, there was a persistent feeling of something else there. This brings up the question of what, or who, exactly are Saints?

In Italian-American folk magic, and in my practice especially, I see the Saints not just through the doctrine and the institution of the Church, but through a lens of familial and local culture and belief. Saints are humans who lived—this allows them to understand certain aspects of our human experience that inhuman entities like deities may not—but in death, many of them have become channels for something older.

Saints, as Dee Norman writes in *Burn a Black Candle: An Italian American Grimoire* are,

> *In the simplest sense, saints are people who are considered to have lived particularly holy lives... Someone who isn't a devout Catholic...understands that a saint is an entity with distinct areas of expertise or interest. In my eyes, whether a saint started out as a physical living being or not, they represent a force that humans can work with. I can use information about the saint's time on Earth or stories about the miracles they performed after death to understand the kind of entity/force that is behind the saintly image (120).*

In reference to the syncretism with Catholicism and the folk magic of Italy and Italian-Americans, Lisa Fazio in *Della Medicina* quotes Andrea Romanazzi,

> *Folk conjuration is not...very different from the magic formulas of antiquity. For the people...the saints are divinities, the result of a real coexistence/communion between an ancient polytheism and the new monotheistic religions, perhaps too far from the needs and necessities of man...all this has nothing to do with Christian prayers with which, due to the similarity of figures, magic can be confused. In fact, if prayer is a move to petition the divine, whoever it is, the conjuration has within itself the power of the magical evocative force. It is a short prayer that contains this divine sprak from which the divinity can not escape (194).*

Lisa Fazio continues, "Segnature and all of the elements of Italian folk medicine that are merged with Catholicism contain, at their origins, the roots of a life and a world much more primordial" (195).

In my opinion and experience, both answers have the capability to be correct. Many different traditions have been syncretized with

Catholicism and utilized Saints as "faces" for entities and spirits that have existed earlier. Folk magic, folk beliefs, and long-standing religions and traditions do not just disappear when a colonizing force asks them too—they adapt. They change. They syncretize. There are many Saints I work with as Catholic entities and as people who lived and died. Still, I see different primordial energies operating through them. If we cannot access resources, the symbolism around Saints often tells us more about what the Saint may be associated with. Saint Expedite, well known in folk traditions for his quick action, red colors, and love for poundcake, is a Saint with a very Mercurial energy. He is associated with a crow and was a Roman soldier whose appearance in folk magic seems relatively inexplicable. Santa Lucia, celebrated in both Sicily and Sweden, is known for being the patron Saint of eyesight and the blind. She carries her eyes on a plate and a fern frond, and her celebration during some of the darkest months often utilizes light and candles. In Sweden, Santa Lucia is associated with Lucifer, the Light Bringer. This may be due to her name, from its Latin origin. The Virgin Mary is long associated with many different ancient goddesses, including Isis, Diana, Juno, and other entities ruling over childbirth, mothers, and women.

Despite what you may think about what Saints are or aren't, a question still stands; if these are Catholic entities, how can we possibly work with them as non-Catholics? Saints are far from singularly Catholic entities—they exist in many different religions and contexts across the world. They are, in my opinion, mostly relatively kind spirits wanting to help those who come to them—especially those whose ancestors they may have had a rapport with. Five years into my reconnection journey, I still don't consider myself a Catholic. If anything, I am a folk Catholic, a term which I refer to as a worldview that centers the people in Catholicism rather the institution. It asks us to look at how we can form relationships with Saints and holy beings without human intercession. It encourages us to center folk magic and the needs of the people rather than the dictations of those appointed as leaders by an institution. There are many folks who would call themselves traditional Catholics that I would consider folk Catholics. There are also many individuals who say they are folk Catholics that I would argue are more traditional. Terms float around and are created and destroyed continuously, and this is something the folk practitioner must take in stride. I consider myself a folk Catholic because I don't go to Church except when I need to get some holy water or maybe on important holidays. I don't utilize the Bible to ensure that I am a good person. I don't believe you have to atone for sins to get into Heaven, if it exists, and I don't agree with many people's idea of what sin is. I trust myself and my community to be responsible and moral because being a good person shouldn't come with an asterisk. I don't evangelize, I don't preach, and I don't think that Christianity is for everyone, nor should everyone seek out Jesus.

More traditional Catholics may argue that a non-Catholic utilizing Catholic elements in a heretical context is blasphemy, yet the Catholic Church has spent the majority of its history attempting to convert multiple different ethnic groups, demonizing and criminalizing Indigenous spiritualities, and forcing many different communities and ethnic groups into Catholicism to receive the support they need. The Catholic Church, as a colonizing force, does not hold much sway over how the folks it holds influence over utilize its tools, nor does it have a large say in the reclamation of Catholic elements within particular cultural contexts and folk magics. The Americanized ideals of Christianity appear to differ greatly from those in the Italian context—the culture which informs the diasporic community of Italian-Americans who continue the long-standing tradition of the cult of the saints.

Asking whether a folk practitioner who does not identify as Catholic, yet works with Saints, believes in G-d or not is a perfectly acceptable avenue of thought. Yet, I would argue that my particular folk practice doesn't tend to concern themselves with questions of the divine or how the universe works. Folk magic surrounds the magic that the folk need—which may not just be magical remedies for situations. We can muse on bigger ideas like who the Saints are, why it works when we petition them, who they are talking to—yet none of us truly know the answer. In many ways, I think the best question to ask is not "Do you believe in the Christian G-d?", but "Does this work for you?"

It is not lost on me that I am not a Catholic—in the same way that it is not lost on me that I am not truly a pagan. While many would argue that my practice is pagan due to its fringe or niche way of approaching the spiritual world, it does not fit into the typical neopagan ideas we've seen dominating the mainstream publications and books. Aspects of it are certainly pagan through the word's historical usage, meaning non-Christian. Yet there are many non-Christian religions and spiritualities that are not pagan. I invoke Mercury as a god in the same breath as invoking Saint Expedite. I call upon Diana utilizing the rosary. The Catholic elements of my practice, from the view of someone who has never been within Italian-American folk magic, are nonsensical.

The term "dual faith" was originally introduced to me by my friend Mahigan Saint-Pierre, owner of Kitchen Toad, who borrowed it from anthropological texts, but conversations on dual faith and mixtures of faith have been occurring for years within our occult and folk magic community. In 2022, Joanna Tarnawska, who runs the Polish Folk Witch account, writes of responses to dual faith,

> *Pagan witches argue that they have no idea how a fellow witch can accept oppressive Abrahamic and monotheistic elements in their craft. Instead, they generally strive to "disinfect" their ancestral traditions from any and all post-Christianization elements. Christian witches, on the other hand, argue that dual faith is no longer needed, and thus no longer valid, because in modern times there is no inquisition and no witch hunts going on; they would argue that one is safer to embrace either Christian craft or pagan craft instead of mixing the two.*

Further expanding that,

> *What both of these groups fail to understand is that dual faith does not equal Christianity, and that folk Catholicism does not equal*

Catholicism, and—perhaps shockingly—it is not monotheism. Folk Catholicism is not an official religion, it does not adhere to the rules of the church and, in fact, often actively goes against such rules and hierarchies, as is broadly documented in the multitude of heretical folk magic practices that have to do with stealing the host, summoning the devil in the churchyard, and many others. The folk witch is known for sitting in the first row during Sunday mass, and simultaneously speaking with the Devil on a Saturday night in the church's backyard.

Yvonne Aburrow writes of dual faith on her blog, "Dowsing with Divinity," in the same year. She quotes Stephen Hayes, who identifies several reasons why "an encounter between a missionizing religion and an indigenous one" may exist:

1. **Rejection.** The traditional knowledge is rejected as purely evil.
2. ***Dvoeverie.*** Two incompatible beliefs or worldviews are held side by side, with little or no interaction between them.
3. **Syncretism**. The two different beliefs are mingled, to make a third, and new belief, which is different from either component.
4. **Inculturation**. Where the original local culture is transformed, and the incoming belief becomes part of it (Aburrow).

Within this framework, a variety of ideas and systems have the capability to take root. Some may require a full transition away from traditional knowledge. Others may be completely incompatible, yet exist next to each other nonetheless. Others may mingle and create a third belief. In many ways, folk Catholicism and other folk beliefs surrounding a mix between religion and magic that the religion disagrees with do exist. Dual faith, in many ways, refers to two religions or ways of being held next to each other in varying degrees—as adversaries, as mingling beliefs, as transformation. The cult of the saints in Italian-American folk magic seems to be a prime representation of syncretism, yet also of *dvoeverie.* Many practitioners in this tradition that I know of work with Saints, but also may work with Roman or Greek gods. They venerate spirits of the land and of our dead. They perform rituals and acts that the Church disagrees with. They may recognize Saints as earlier beings or they may not, and they may utilize prayers, folk medicine, and celebrate holidays in ways that give a nod to earlier, pre-Christian traditions.

This phenomenon doesn't just exist with Italian-American culture, but also within:

> *The interaction of Buddhism and Shinto. According to Kuroda, Shinto was not a distinct religion prior to the arrival of Buddhism (Shinto was originally a Chinese word signifying any and all folk religion in China, Korea and Japan). In Japan, it is possible to be both Buddhist and Shinto at the same time, because neither world-view necessarily denies the other. This is perhaps similar to Hayes' model of inculturation, whereby the incoming tradition transforms the indigenous one (though I suspect the process is actually one of mutual transformation) (Aburrow).*

In the context of this, Yvonne continues, quoting another source, A.W. Woodburne, "a need is felt to make some form of accommodation with the truth claims of the other religion, sometimes by denying them, sometimes by recasting them in the language of one's own tradition, and sometimes by assigning the other religion's holy figure a position in one's own tradition; for example, Hindus regarding Jesus as a 'supremely religious soul.'"

Dual faith, in its essence, is two beliefs interacting with each other in a way that does not always make sense to those who have not been exposed to the syncretism and integration of these beliefs. For those within the cultural context, these ways of being are natural or second nature. This is how I often respond to those asking me the bigger questions. I'm unsure if I even care if the Christian God is the force that I am working with through the Saints—rather, I care that it works. I care that I receive a response in my time of need—that when I place petitions under the feet of Saint Anthony or Saint

Expedite, they are fulfilled. Folk Catholic elements in my practice tend to mirror other spirit relationships, with the distinguishing signature being that I typically utilize more Christian methods to work with Saints. This could be praying a novena, a nine-day prayer, to them, or using specific prayers formulated to insert a petition. Still, I approach these Saints outside the Church. When I am in need, I don't attend a mass—rather, I go to the altar of the Saint within my home and place a prayer or petition under the feet of the statue. I work with specific Saints in spellwork that is certainly not Catholic. By all definitions, I am a heretic to the Church and a Catholic to the pagan community, but my practice and relationship exists within a space that is only beginning to be acknowledged by the wider witchcraft and occult sphere. Dual faith and folk magic exist in the liminal and the in-between, often operating off of cultural contexts that one who is outside of it may not understand, through syncretism and through survival.

My practice, at its core, exists by honoring those who came before me. While I see a link to earlier pagan gods in the Saints, many would refuse to acknowledge this. All of my most recent ancestors were good Catholics, even if I feel as though their Catholicism is something a little more. In this conversation, we have to make room for the truth as the person or practitioner experiences it. Rather than insisting that our perspective or idea of Saint work is right, I implore readers to make room for multiple truths. Our ancestors were Catholic, but did things the Church would disagree with. Our Saints may be faces for earlier entities, but they are still Saints. Our practices are heretical and sacred, pagan to the Church and Catholic to the pagans. Both can be true at once. Instead of getting caught up on the labels we or others ascribe to our practice, I encourage you to see what a relationship with Saints would look like outside the institution of the Church. Treat them with respect but approach them like you would any other spirit—as someone in need, as a folk practitioner, as exactly who you are. You may very well receive a response.

Bibliography

Aburrow, Yvonne. "Dual-Faith Practice." *Dowsing for Divinity*, 16 Jan. 2013, https://www.patheos.com/blogs/sermonsfromthe-mound/2013/01/dual-faith-practice-1.

Beauchamp, Zack. "How Italy Became a Country, in One Animated Map." *Vox*, 1 Dec. 2014, https://www.vox.com/2014/12/1/7314717/italian-unification.

Blunt, John J. *Vestiges of Ancient Manners and Customs, Discoverable in Modern Italy and Sicily*. 1823, pp. 120.

Bonfiglio, MaryBeth. "La Befana: Christmas Witch, Goddess of Ancestral Spirit, Fascist Propaganda (+ Befanini Recipe and Spell)." *Radici Siciliane*, 28 Dec. 2019, https://www.radicisiciliane.com/blog/la-befana-christmas-witch-goddess-of-ancestral-spirit-fascist-propaganda-befanini-recipe-and-spell.

Brady, M. Michael. "The Light and Dark Origins of Lucia." *The Norwegian American*, 31 Dec. 2020, https://www.norwegianamerican.com/the-light-and-dark-origins-of-lucia/.

Churcher, Connie. "Saint Lucia's Day." *Horniman Museum and Gardens*, 9 Dec. 2021, https://www.horniman.ac.uk/story/saint-lucias-day/#:~:text=In%20Sweden%2C%20Lucia%20is%20also,had%20children%20with%20the%20devil.

Crisis, Karyn. *Italian Magic: Secret Lives of Women*. Karyn Krol-Tiso, 2020.

Fahrun, Mary-Grace. *Italian Folk Magic: Rue's Kitchen Witchery*. Red Wheel/Weiser, 2018.

Fazio, Lisa. *Della Medicina: The Tradition of Italian-American Folk Healing*. Simon and Schuster, 2024, pp. 194-195.

"Italian Playing Cards: Traditional & Regional Decks." *Understanding Italy*, 1 Oct. 2022, https://www.understandingitaly.com/cards.html.

Malbrough, Ray T. *The Magical Power of Saints: Evocation and Candle Rituals*. Llewellyn+Orm, 2014.

Malpezzi, Frances M., and William M. Clements. *Italian-American Folklore*. August House, 1992, pp. 116.

Norman, Dee. *Burn a Black Candle: An Italian American Grimoire.* National Geographic Books, 2022, pp. 120.

Open Theology. *St. Anthony in Quimbanda.* ResearchGate, 2023, https://www.researchgate.net/figure/St-Anthony-in-Quimbanda-Collection-of-the-Templo-de-Kimbanda-Dominio-do-Exu-Marabo-e_fig2_371005140.

Puca, Angela. *Italian Witchcraft and Shamanism: The Tradition of Segnature, Indigenous and Trans-Cultural Shamanic Traditions in Italy.* BRILL, 2024.

Rozett, Ella. "Montevergine." *Interfaith Mary*, 20 Aug. 2017, https://www.interfaithmary.net/black-madonna-index/montevergine.

Tarnawaska, Joanna. "Dual Faith: The Elephant in the Room of the Witchcraft Community | Polish Folk Witch." *Patreon*, 7 Sept. 2023, www.patreon.com/posts/dual-faith-in-of-88905580.

Taumaturgo, Agostino. *The Things We Do: Ways of the Holy Benedetta.* Createspace Independent Publishing Platform, 2007, pp. 117.

Vaudoise, Mallorie. "Madonna of the Mountain in Polsi, Calabria." *Italian Folk Magic*, 12 May 2017, https://www.italian folkmagic.com/blog/2017/5/12/madonna-of-the-mountain-in-polsi-calabria.

Living the Sacred Calendar

Spiritual and Magical Practices of the Contemporary Maya

by Kenneth Johnson

It's pleasant to relax and enjoy the sunlight down in the Maya lands. You can hang out forever in expatriate centers like Lake Atitlan or Antigua. You can meet local sages in colorful clothes who will use their best "school" Spanish to "speak New Age" with you. They will use familiar words like "harmonic" or "resonance." And of course they will use everyone's favorite word, "galactic." (And I hate to rain on anyone's parade, but that word cannot be found in any dictionary for any of the thirty existing Mayan languages.)

You know you are entering a different world altogether when you travel to a place where the only way to reach your destination is the chicken bus. Everyone is stuffed like sardines into a rickety old bus with the brand name "Bluebird." This is the bus company of choice for U.S. school systems; when whole fleets of buses are decommissioned because of old age, they are sold to Guatemala. They are so ancient that you begin to wonder if you might actually have gone to grade school on that very bus. You're hanging onto the luggage rack for dear life but unable to move due to the sheer number of human bodies.

The driver races madly around blind mountain curves; you will be thoroughly convinced that the elaborate shrine he has constructed upon the dashboard is an absolute necessity for survival. One needs the assistance of any saint who's willing to dish it out.

At last, you reach your destination. The first thing you notice, which differs so radically from Antigua or Lake Atitlan, is that no one is approaching you and trying to sell you trinkets, beads, or native clothing which won't fit anyone you know.

In fact, no one is approaching you at all.

When I first arrived in Momostenango, it was a market day. Even as I trundled through the town square with my luggage, I was quickly aware of the fact that no one was speaking Spanish anymore. There was only K'iche'. From the very beginning, you're lost, without an anchor. Not a single word makes any sense to you. Children hide behind their mothers' skirts and stare at you with wide open eyes, and sometimes with obvious fear. The mothers themselves turn away and won't look at you. You know that they are from the villages and have only come into town for the market; unlike the townsfolk who pay no heed to the ubiquitous stream of Mormon missionaries with their close-cropped blond hair and standard issue white shirts with short sleeves, the villagers are completely unaccustomed to the sight of foreigners.

Entering town on the bus, my first impression was that Momostenango, so celebrated by anthropologists for its traditional ways, looked absolutely, relentlessly ordinary. Had I been driving through without knowing its history or reputation, I would have noticed nothing the least bit unusual about it. A typical Guatemalan town.

But as I walked through the plaza and the *mercado*, I began to get the impression that I had inadvertently misadventured into a region not of light, but of darkness. Half the population appeared to be dressed in rags. Eyes were hollow with poverty and hunger. Girls scarcely sixteen shuffled across the plaza, their backs bent and burdened with enormous loads of firewood, sporting a baby on each hip. Drunks lurched out of cantinas with the zombie-like stare that only comes from drinking that wretched Quetzalteca liqueur—whatever the distillation process may be, it would certainly be illegal in most nations. The drunks swayed, puked, and tumbled into the streets in front of oncoming cars. (Later, the day keeper Don Rigoberto would say to me: "In your country, did the government not license the whiskey traders to frequent the frontier forts where Indians gathered, keep them drunk and stupid so they wouldn't revolt? Colonial oppression is just the same wherever you go.")

A dilapidated pickup truck lumbered by. In the back were three *campesinos* and a dead cow. The cow was enormous; bigger than all three farmers put together. Every inch of it was intact, except for the fact that its hide had been removed, leaving the entire cow as a mass of bright pink epidermis shining, fly-blown, in the sun. Having sold the hide, they were presumably now on their way to the butcher.

No wonder the famous "city of the day keepers" wasn't a big item on the tourist circuit.

I reached the *jardin* in front of the civic administrative buildings. The guards were falling asleep holding Soviet issue AK-47s that were so old they would surely blow up in the shooter's face rather than cause harm to any bandits. An out of tune Latin band blared wearily from a rickety gazebo in the *jardin.*

Could this really be "sacred Momostenango," the heart and soul of Mayan Calendar traditionalism?

In a sense, it is no longer necessary to come all the way to Momos in order to study the ancient calendar. In a sense, it never was. Many communities in the highlands of Guatemala still govern their religious lives in accordance with the 260-day cycle which is called the *ch'ol q'ij* in K'iche' or, more familiarly to most, the *tzolk'in* in Yucatec. Anthropological studies on the practice of the ancient calendar as a spiritual path had been written about Chichicastenango and Todos Santos years before Barbara Tedlock wrote her now-legendary *Time and the Highland Maya* in Momos. And when the Maya were granted their religious freedom by way of the Peace Accords in December, 1996, which ended the horrors of the Guatemalan civil war, a return to the ancient traditions began to spread like wildfire throughout the Mayan world, as the disconnected and the dis-enculturated started to reclaim their ancient roots, to reclaim what it meant to be Maya.

But despite the rebirth of the ancient calendar and all its associated spiritual practices throughout Guatemala and even beyond, Momostenango remained "special." It was here, more than anywhere, that the Maya had tenaciously, sometimes even rebelliously, held on to their traditions throughout five hundred years of colonialism. The ancient rites and ceremonies were more elaborate in Momos than anywhere else, the adherence to the practices associated with the sacred days more rigorously kept. It wasn't necessary to go all the way to Momos—with its poverty, its drunks, and its hardships—in order to learn the ways of the ancient calendar. But I have lived my life by extremes rather than by half measures, and for me nothing would serve my purpose except a return to the source.

In the course of time, I came to see that life in such traditional environments is just that—traditional. One day is pretty much the same as another. The men rise early and go to work, whether performing manual labor for an overlord or farming their own cornfields. The women rise even earlier; they cook and look after the children. There are no hospitals. There are only a few doctors. The most respected citizens in town are the midwives. Changes in the daily routine consist of births, marriages, and deaths.

Thus, in time, one begins to move to a different rhythm. The rhythm of the *ch'ol q'ij*, or ancient calendar.

In Momostenango, people are likely to say, "Today is 4 I'x, isn't it?" in precisely the same way that we would say, "Today is Tuesday, isn't it?" The Mayan Calendar is that common and that well known; I am not exaggerating.

Many have said that the Mayan Calendar is a road, a path. And this is true. While most day keepers or Indigenous priests in

Momostenango do believe that various astronomical and cosmic cycles are embodied in the *chol q'ij,* the principal metaphor is that of the road, the path, specifically the path that we walk as we grow for nine months in our mother's womb, the path from gestation to full birth, full participation in the human world.

But there is a major difference between our cultural conception of "the path" and that which is conceived by the Maya. We tend to see the "spiritual path" as something we walk by ourselves, as if we were lonely pilgrims, crossing a vast mountain range with staff in hand, guided only by a star or an inner voice.

To the Maya, we never walk the path alone. Each and every day connects us with another important part of the world around us, and it is this wider, more extended world which constitutes the real spiritual "path."

On Aj (Day of the Cornstalk) days, we give thanks for the children and the animals in our environment. On I'x (Jaguar) days, we honor sacred places, such as rocks, mountaintops, and springs of living water. Ajmaq (Trickster) days and Ajpu (Hunter) days are for remembering our ancestors, those who have walked before us upon the path, and who have now walked on into the next world. Aq'ab'al (Day of the Dawning) days are for lovers, and Kawoq (no existing translation) days for the women in our lives and environment (especially the midwives and the healers). Q'anil (Ripening) days are for honoring plants and flowers, for giving thanks to the earth that supplies us with crops. There are indeed days when it is appropriate to focus on issues having to do with the self—E' (the Road of Life) is the day of our personal destiny, Tz'ikin (Eagle) is the day upon which we pray for material prosperity, and No'j (Thought) is the day to clarify our thinking. But even the days that are about "us" may serve, in many ways, to place "us" in context with everything around us. The emphasis is always on relatedness, connectedness. There is no room in a Mayan community for the kind of introspective self-absorption that we commonly associate with the spiritual quest. If your inner child is demanding all your attention, maybe it's just plain cranky and in need of a "time out."

To step into the rhythm of the Mayan Calendar is to become intimately connected with the entire world that surrounds us, in all its beauty and its glory. The Tzutujil Maya of Lake Atitlan speak of our Earth as the "Blossoming World." It is our duty and our privilege to participate fully in the magic and wonder of this Blossoming World—to be "cooked in the oven of human existence" until we emerge warm and tasty and delicious. This cannot be done by turning away from society, sitting alone on a mountaintop, enjoying neither food nor love. Among the Maya, that would be considered anti-social behavior rather than holiness. If your uncle gets drunk and falls off the back of the pick-up truck, you don't write him a convoluted letter explaining why you are much too sensitive to deal with dysfunctional relationships in your life. You just pick him up, load him back on the truck, and keep going. After all, he too is part of the Blossoming World. He too will someday become one of the ancestors who look back upon us with joy from every sunset and every stream.

If you stay in Momos long enough, you begin to wait in anticipation of favorite ceremonial days. It's 8 B'atz' (Monkey), so now we will initiate the shamans. There will actually be some guests at the local hotel. Maybe even foreigners! On Tz'ikin days, the shops that sell magical supplies will have laid in their stock of sugar dyed green in anticipation of the prosperity ceremonies that are held on that day.

For me, there was a time when the esoteric talk and the ceremonies started to seem less formal. It all began to feel more like a family party. That's how I knew I had finally entered the flow of sacred time which is the *ch'ol q'ij*. In time, one even learns to catch some of the local dialect, the common mix of Spanish and K'iche' that the women speak while working in the kitchen:

"Pablo really likes Angela."

"All the boys like Angela. She was born on a Aq'ab'al day. You know how romantic they are!"

"Yes, but Pablo is Kan (Serpent). And you know how silent those serpents are. He will never tell her how he feels!"

Now, not suddenly but gradually, everything becomes different. The ceremonies, the teaching conversations, the rhythm of sacred time—it was no longer a distant and formal affair but had become a part of my everyday life.

Sometimes you know what day it is even if you have forgotten to count. I can remember walking outdoors on certain mornings and seeing plumes of smoke rising from behind the walls of the nearby cemetery as *costumbristas* (traditionalists) lit fires at the graves of their ancestors. And you say to yourself: "Must be an Ajpu day." You know this because you know that Ajpu is the day when they honor the ancestors.

Finally, it reaches the point where the difference between "ordinary time" and "sacred time" disappears altogether. One begins to move to a different rhythm, to dance to an unaccustomed music.

Finally, you are living on Mayan time.

The calendar creates a time frame of its own. Each day has its meaning.

It is not a deterministic way of life; it is not a kind of fatalism, as if any given event was supposed to "happen" on such and such day. Rather, it is a question of performing actions that are appropriate to the symbolic significance of the day. It doesn't matter whether such actions are comprised of specific rituals and ceremonies to be performed at the top of Cerro Paklom or at some other shrine, whether such actions are perfectly ordinary human concerns such as opening a business, taking a bus trip, or scheduling the working hours in one's cornfield. The *ch'ol q'ij* is "sacred time" rather than ordinary time; when we align ourselves with its rhythm, we live in a sacred way, no matter how ordinary our deeds may appear.

After seven years of frequent and lengthy visits to Momostenango, the time finally arrived for me to become initiated as a day keeper.

It was unexpected. My friend and traveling companion, Susi, had gone for a visit to Victoria, a midwife who also had a sterling reputation as an herbalist, day keeper, ritualist, and all-around healer. Susi had health problems, perhaps Victoria could help her.

The form of divination favored by the Maya involves opening one's *vara sagrada,* the sacred medicine bag received during one's initiation, and placing its contents—260 red seeds of the *tz'ite,* or wild coral tree, as well as assorted crystals—on a cloth, then emptying one's mind while grasping a handful of seeds. The seeds are laid out upon the cloth in groups of four, and each group is regarded as one of the days of the calendar. One counts the days; the final days in the spread will symbolize the answer to one's question.

Victoria told Susi that those born on Tijax (Obsidian Blade) days were natural healers, but that they typically discovered their healing talents by experiencing an illness. Those born upon Tijax cannot simply go to a healer and seek out healing; they must learn how to heal themselves, and then they can fulfill their destiny by going on to heal others. When Susi told Victoria that she knew nothing of healing, Victoria just shrugged her shoulders and said, "Well then, I shall have to train you. You will take initiation as a day keeper from me, and your specialty shall be healing."

I had seen a fair number of *tz'ite* readings, though I did not do them myself; one must be an initiated day keeper in order to practice the divination ritual. I was impressed by Victoria's clarity and her command of the art; a few days later I sought her out with a problem of my own. For the last few years, my life had been an endless litany of financial problems, estrangement with close relatives, and several bad relationships. I had always been taught that the *nawales* (the K'iche' term for the day signs of the calendar, borrowed from the Nahuatl language) were living spiritual entities, not just symbols, and if they felt you disrespected them, they could make your life quite difficult. I had begun to wonder if perhaps some of the information I had written in my books about the Maya was inaccurate, and the *nawales* were angry and intended to give me hell about it. I asked Victoria. She took my question quite seriously, then cast the seeds. "No," she said, "it is just the opposite. It has always been your destiny to become a day keeper, and you have not gotten round to it yet, so the *nawales* are simply trying to wake you up."

"No one has offered me initiation," I replied.

"Well then, I will initiate you. It is best if you and your friend are initiated together. People are initiated in a solitary way nowadays, but the old-fashioned way was to initiate a woman and a man at the same time."

So there it was. Susi Lötscher and I were to become day keepers, *aj q'ijab.*

But first, we would have to be purified with a ritual called a *saturácion,* in which one is literally saturated with positive healing energy, a complete karmic clean-out to leave you empty and reborn for the new road ahead.

Some days later, Susi and I waited at dawn on the steps of the church in the village of San Jorge la Laguna, on the shores of Lake Atitlan. A *tuk-tuk* came rolling into the plaza. (A *tuk-tuk* is a form of Guatemalan public transport which has been called a "motorized rickshaw." It could also be described as an exalted golf cart.) Victoria's daughter, Lidia, stepped out of the *tuk-tuk* and motioned for us to join her. We all squeezed into the contraption and the driver took us to the top of the village, where a stone wall protected a cliff that dropped steeply down to the lake. Victoria was waiting for us there. She had two large boxes of ceremonial materials with her. Clearly, this was going to be a substantial ritual.

We began to make our way down the cliff. The rocky dirt trail was steep. Even though I was raised in a family devoted to hiking and camping, I sometimes felt unsure of my footing and wondered if I would slip and tumble all the way down to the lake. Victoria and Lidia simply removed their shoes, stuffed them in their bags, and proceeded to walk barefoot down the hill with great ease, each one balancing one of the boxes on her head.

Soon, we reached a cave in the mountainside. It was called Nimajay. The entrance to the cave was filled with the ashes of previous ceremonial fires, and there were many candles, rows of them standing up amid the ashes. The first thing Victoria did was to hand us some candles and instruct us to plant the candles and name them for some of our relatives who had passed over. When we had completed that phase, we lit the candles.

Then Victoria and Lidia constructed the altar. The ritual which is known as a Fire Ceremony is the foundation stone of Mayan spiritual practice. Almost any other, including our *saturación,* is a variation on the basic Fire Ceremony.

A Mayan altar begins with a hieroglyphic symbol for the day-sign Q'anil laid out upon the ground with sugar (which symbolizes the sweetness of life), then offerings are piled upon it.

Offerings may include candles, flowers, copal incense in various forms, *ocote* wood, *pericone* (wild marigold), rosemary, and, almost always, cigarettes or cigars. (If one studies Classical Mayan art, it will be noticed that ancestral spirits living in the Underworld are always depicted smoking cigars, and indeed the tobacco was an offering to the spirits of the ancestors.)

Then the guardians of the four directions are invoked and the fire is lit. As the fire begins to rise, the officiating day keeper, or *aj q'ij,* recites a prayer from the Popol Vuh, the Mayan Creation Epic. In the prayer, a new World Age has been created, but as yet there is no Sun, no Moon. The First People wander through the dark, praying for light:

Thou Maker, thou Modeler, look at us, listen to us,
don't let us fall, don't leave us aside, thou god in the sky,
on the earth, Heart of Sky, Heart of Earth,
Give us our sign, our word,
as long as there is day, as long as there is light.
When it comes to the sowing, the dawning,
will it be a greening road, a greening path?
Give us a steady light, a level place, a good light, a good place,
a good life and beginning.
Give us all of this, thou Hurricane, Newborn Thunderbolt,
Raw Thunderbolt, Newborn Nanahuac,

Raw Nanahuac, Falcon, Hunahpu,
Sovereign Plumed Serpent, Bearer, Begetter,
Xpiyacoc, Xmucane,
Grandmother of Day, Grandmother of Light,
when it comes to the sowing, the dawning.[1]

The 260 days of the calendar are counted out—not sequentially as in 1 No'j, 2 Tijax, 3 Kawoq, and so on, but in abbreviated form: 1 No'j, 2 No'j, 3 No'j, 4 No'j, and so on, up to thirteen, and then Tijax is counted out in the same fashion.

Because it was a *saturación,* our ceremony was much lengthier than a typical Fire Ceremony. The smoke stung our eyes, and we often had to step outside of the smoky mouth of the cave to breathe the fresh air rising from the lake. We were given any number of healing substances to hold close to us—bags of the cake-like copal called *pom ensarte,* slabs of hardened molasses, chamomile for the stomach and rue for the mind.... On and on it went for two hours, with Victoria sometimes calling out to us to check the candles and see which ones among our ancestors were here with us.

In the end, there occurred a phenomenon I had never seen before in all my years of visiting Guatemala. A clump of herbs and candles, all burning together in the fire, began to form itself into a wreath, and the wreath rose up until it appeared to be standing upright. Victoria said it was a good sign. Susi and I, never having seen anything quite like it, had to agree.

Finally, the *saturácion* was done. We were ready to begin our training as day keepers.

However, contrary to popular belief, initiation is not always as simple as a big dose of *ayahuasca* and a few lonesome days in the wilderness without a steak dinner or even a Big Mac. Mayan initiation

---

1 Tedlock 169–70

entails a long period of intellectual study. The traditional time frame (often altered now for *gringos,* though it was not so for us) is 260 days, a complete round of the ancient calendar. One studies all the details of the Mayan cosmovision and becomes familiar with the Popol Vuh. One must practice reading the *tz'ite* seeds in order to master the divination ritual. While it is true that one is not allowed to work with the seeds themselves until initiation, there are a number of substitutes with which one may practice. Corn kernels work nicely, as do dried kidney beans.

But most of all, one focuses upon learning how to perform a Fire Ceremony correctly. We were able to practice easily while we were in Guatemala, but for part of the time we were at Susi's home in Switzerland. Things were different there. What was completely normal in Guatemala could result in one's being arrested for starting a fire without a city permit, defacing public or private property, and possibly creating a public nuisance. At times we were able to access a plot in one of the community gardens; I dug a fire pit for us there. Other gardeners who observed our ceremonies did not always gaze upon us with friendly faces, however; we sometimes had to create miniaturized substitute ceremonies at home.

The time came for us to return to Guatemala and undergo the initiation rituals. Susi went first, as she was born on a Tijax day and 8 Tijax occurred at just the right time. I went three days later, on 11 Imox because I was born on an Imox (Crocodile) day.

As with Susi's initiation, my own began at dawn when we arrived once again at Victoria's house. I knelt on the floor as Victoria's other daughter, Virginia, tied the *pañuelo* around my head. (The Maya practice one of the many mystical traditions which cover the crown chakra during spiritual work.) Then she handed me my *vara sagrada.*

Possession of a *vara sagrada* is what makes one a day keeper. Basically, it is a bag containing 260 seeds of the *tz'ite* tree, a species of wild coral. *Tz'ite* seeds are bright red and look like small pieces of coral. They are commonly mixed with small pieces of crystal, as well as with several larger crystals. The seeds and small crystals will be used for divination. The bag is wrapped in a cloth called an *envoltorio,* which will be used in the divination ritual as a cloth on which to lay out one's divining seeds. The larger crystals, though not specifically used for divination, are arranged on the cloth, typically in meaningful patterns.

Those who are familiar with Spanish will wonder at the name *vara sagrada,* for the term *vara* is generally used to describe a walking staff. The late Humberto Ak'abal, Guatemala's most renowned poet and a Momostecan whom I came to know during my visits there, explained to me that *vara* was, in this case, just a local dialectical pronunciation of *barata,* which refers to a deck of cards used in divination and featured characters such as The Guardian Angel, The Devil, The Mermaid, The Drunk, and so on. Therefore, the term *vara sagrada* means "sacred divining equipment."

In my initiation ceremony, Virginia was playing the role of the *madrina.* This Spanish word can mean either mother-in-law or bridesmaid, and both are relevant to the ceremony. Your *vara sagrada* is regarded as your spiritual spouse. This is why day keepers often refrain from sexual activity before performing spiritual work. One wishes one's spiritual spouse to be functioning at the highest possible level—and not wracked with jealousy about your worldly spouse. So, one ought to maintain distance from one's worldly spouse before an important ritual. (In the old days, day keepers abstained for as long as a week, but we all live in the modern world now, and twenty-four hours has become customary.) The *madrina* gathers the seeds and crystals and creates your *vara sagrada*—hence she is the mother of your spiritual spouse, your mother-in-law. She also presents you with the *vara sagrada,* thus playing the role of bridesmaid as well.

Victoria lit four fires, and I was told to make prayers over all of them, specifically to my ancestors.

By the time we were finished with that part of the ceremony, our guests and Victoria's team of assistants had all arrived, and it was time for us to begin our journey to the five sacred altars of Momostenango.

In former days, everyone walked the circuit of the altars, and the majority of initiates still do. But Victoria, growing older, was not as fond of long walks as she used to be, and so we rode in a van, which two members of our team were driving.

We drove up the dirt road of a steep hill, for the first altar was also the town's highest, Nima Sabal. From that vantage point, one could look out upon the whole landscape, for miles around. On December 21, 2012, Nima Sabal was the place where Victoria's brother-in-law, Rigoberto Itzep Chanchavac, had chosen to re-create the ceremony described in the Popol Vuh in which the First People, wandering in darkness, reach the top of a hill, and there they witness the sunrise of the new World Age, and do ceremony accordingly. And it is here, on the day 9 B'atz', that the whole town turns out to take part in a series of rituals that honor the Divine Feminine principle in nature. Nine is an important number, for it symbolizes women, the ancestors, and life in general (for we all spend nine months in the womb of our mother).

We performed our first Fire Ceremony at Nima Sabal, and we—Victoria, Virginia, and I—would perform ceremony at each of the five sacred altars. The purpose of these ceremonies is to introduce the new initiate and their *vara sagrada* to the spirit guardians of each of the altars.

After the ceremony, we drove back down the hill to the central part of the town, where we visited Chuti Sabal, the altar that is sacred to the number eight. In Mayan numerology, eight is a powerful and important number, and that numbered day is most often preferred for ritual. The day upon which the K'iche' Maya initiate new shamans is 8 B'atz'. The day upon which they initiate a *chuchq'ajaw,* or "mother-father," the highest level of the shamanic priesthood, is 8 Kej (Deer). Despite the deep significance of the number eight, the altar of Chuti Sabal had always appeared to be a peaceful and serene, although quite active, shrine. And so it was on that day. We did our ceremony, returned to the car, and moved on to a place which had always had a special magic for me, the altar called Pa Ja.

Pa Ja means "the place of water." There is a meadow, and a stream runs through it. The shrines stand at one side of the meadow.

This is the altar dedicated to the number one. Here, at the beginning of each *trecena* or thirteen-day cycle, the day keepers come and gather water from the stream in glass jars, vials, or whatever they may have. All things begin with water, and it is over a body of water (which probably signifies Lake Atitlan) that the gods gather at the beginning of the Popol Vuh to create the first World Age. The water gathered by the day keepers on every "1" day will later be used in various ceremonies. One could describe it as a kind of "holy water," although one quite different from Catholic holy water. It comes from a fresh stream that flows to the east, the direction of new beginnings.

As I have written, Pa Ja has always had a special magic for me. But I had never mentioned this fact to Victoria, and I was pleasantly surprised when she told me, "Place your *vara sagrada* right here. Pa Ja is its home altar."

While the circuit of the five sacred altars is intended to introduce the initiate and his or her *vara sagrada* to the guardian spirits of the sacred place, there is always one place that is special—the one which is called your home altar, where your *vara sagrada* is in its rightful place. I have no idea how Victoria knew of my affinity for Pa Ja. It has been suggested to me that perhaps she chose it simply because I was born on an Imox day, and Imox is associated with water, especially with the original ocean from which all things are created and in which the primordial crocodile sleeps with the World Tree growing from its back. In any case, I was happy to consecrate my *vara sagrada* to Pa Ja as its home altar.

The day was beginning to wane, and we still had two more altars to visit.

Paklom is unique. It is on a hilltop in the center of town and looks out upon the entire community of Momostenango. It is sacred to the number six, a number known for its strength, stability, and practicality. It is, almost always, the most crowded of all the major altars.

And yet, it is more than that. It is an *omphalos,* a World Center.

It is a common tradition among the Guatemalan Maya that one lives between four sacred mountains. These mountains symbolize the four cardinal directions, and each one is associated with one of the days of the calendar which may serve as the "Lord of the Year." From one culture to another throughout Mesoamerica, different Year Lords were used, but in ancient Tikal as in modern Momostenango, the Year Lords were Kej (East), E' (West), No'j (North), and Iq' (South). The years will be counted as 1 Kej, 2 E', 3 No'j, 4 Iq', 5 Kej, 6 E', and so on, until we have counted thirteen occurrences of each day sign, totaling 52. In 52 years, the calendar will return to its initial beginning place in terms of the day sign, the solar month, and the Year Lord. Thus, our entire Mayan birth pattern recurs when we reach the age of 52, and that landmark signifies our transition into a tribal elder.

This concept of living between four sacred mountains was carried by Toltec merchants to Chaco Canyon, New Mexico, somewhere around 1050 CE. The Pueblo peoples who succeeded the Chaco tradition passed the knowledge to the Navajo, who are now the keepers of the tradition. The mountain of the east is Mt. Blanca, Colorado; in the west it is Humphreys Peak, Arizona; in the north it is Mt. Hesperus, Colorado, and in the south it is Mt. Taylor, New Mexico.

But in order to live surrounded by mountains which symbolize the four directions, one must be at the center, and Paklom—even though it is simply a small hill in the middle of town—is that center. It is the *axis mundi,* the *omphalos,* the sacred center of all things—a shamanic concept recognized throughout the world. The Momostecan "inner universe" of the ancient calendar revolves around Paklom.

But even after visiting the world center, there was still one final altar—the altar known as Kokuch, sacred to the Earth Mother and to the number seven.

Though the Central Mountain, Paklom, was a small place, it was steep; the car rolled down and then into the central plaza of Momostenango. We approached the center. On one side was the cathedral, some hundreds of years old, massive, dominating. On the other side of the center was a small square brick enclosure; this was the altar to the Earth Mother. For hundreds of years now, the people of Momos had been worshiping the Earth Mother right there in the central plaza where the priests—and indeed all those who entered the cathedral—could see them.

This might seem like a somewhat rebellious act on the part of the *costumbristas*—those who still practiced the ancient pre-Christian traditions. The reality of the situation was, in fact, quite different. The Catholic Church had made its peace with the Maya traditionalists long ago. There was even a corner of the cathedral which had been set aside for dual practitioners—those whose spiritual practice was a more or less equal syncretization of Catholicism and *costumbre*—where they could perform their own mixed ceremonies. At this point in time, the only serious threat to ancient tradition came from two sources—one was, of course, evangelical Protestantism, which insisted there could be no friendship between the two paths; the other was the proliferation of cell phones, which display only in Spanish and which were causing the younger citizens of the town to lose their knowledge of K'iche' and, consequently, their knowledge of tradition and their respect for their K'iche' speaking elders.

It was at Kokuch, at sundown, that we performed the last Fire Ceremony of my initiation.

Afterwards, we returned to Victoria's house. She served us a variety of local moonshine which she had created herself. She demonstrated her ability to spray it all the way across the room. She was formidable.

At times, Western culture seems to worship alienation. Our heroes are the "outsiders" of this world, those without a "place to belong." Beginning with the existential loners who have dominated Western literature from Camus and Kerouac, through our fascination with "knights" who hide behind masks and darkness in a cave full of gadgets or "space pirates" with no allegiance to anyone but themselves, we revel in a sense of being solitary and different. And if someone seems to interfere with our quest for self, we can easily break contact with such troublesome characters by refusing to return their messages and claiming that it's necessary for the sake of our "personal growth."

Living in a remote, Indigenous Mayan town, I found all my cherished cultural values completely reversed. One of the words most commonly heard in daily conversation or seen written upon civic announcements was *tinamit,* which means "community." In Mayan society, a sense of community was everything. The goal was not to detach oneself from the collective whole, but to be a part of it.

It begins with one's family. No one spoke of "breaking free" from family ties to forge one's own destiny. An individual path was never entirely separate from the collective path. While one might temporarily go to university or take a job somewhere in the "big city," it was always understood that one's *tinamit* was one's home, and one would return there in the course of time.

Of course, we live in a transient society. The Maya do not. If you asked an average citizen of a Mayan *tinamit* how long her or his family had been in the town, there would be no answer. They have always been there.

Rather than feeling stifled by the bonds that tie them to community and family, they seemed to possess a sense of security which people in our own society lack. There is always a place to go, a place for food and shelter, a place where you will be accepted despite the ups and downs of your personal life. There is always a sense of home, of belonging. Though many people lacked all but the most basic rudiments of survival, there was an assurance that everything would be all right if everyone—family and friends and neighbors—all pulled together to get the job done.

Despite the fact that Guatemala can be a desperately impoverished country—people often walk around the house in semi-darkness because they can't afford to turn on the lights—there was one thing, so common in the United States, that I never saw anywhere in Guatemala.

No one was homeless. The shanty towns of spiritually broken elders living in cardboard boxes and huddling for warmth around trash can fires that are frequently seen lining the streets of one of the world's wealthiest countries were unknown in poverty-stricken Guatemala.

Even the concept of spirituality is marked by the sense of community. Whether through the influence of Christian monasticism or through involvement with various Eastern religions, many of us have been trained to believe that "retreat from the world" is the apex of the spiritual path. The monastery in the clouds, the cave on top of a mountain. There is a perception that such a refuge would be a far better thing than involvement in the mucky, murky world down below.

In Mayan society, such notions of spirituality do not apply. The "spiritual guide" is just that—a guide. To be a guide, one must have people who seek guidance. The spiritual guide is a fully engaged member of the *tinamit,* with a spouse, children, and everything else that creates a sense of belonging. A shaman is one who can counsel and advise others on the path of spiritual harmony because they also strive to live such a path, one that is thoroughly entwined with the community at large—the Maya would probably say "interwoven" rather than "entwined," since many of their metaphors come from the art of weaving.

We, in our psychological and spiritual isolation, often experience a passion for traditional cultures. We may not know why we have the longing to be part of a different or "exotic" world—we only know that the longing is there. Most of those cultures function, as the Maya do, on a principle of inclusiveness where the whole is greater than its parts and where all the members of the community share a common bond and a sense of belonging. Is this, perhaps, what we are really searching for in our endless quests?

Are we simply looking for a place to belong?

Bibliography

Bunzel, Ruth. *Chichicastenango.* J. J. Augustin, 1959.

Oakes, Maud. *The Two Crosses of Todos Santos: Survival of Mayan Religious Ritual.* Bollingen Series, Pantheon, 1951.

Tedlock, Barbara. *Time and the Highland Maya.* University of New Mexico Press, 1992.

Tedlock, Dennis. *Popol Vuh.* Simon & Schuster, 1985.

Journey in Ocha

The Mysteries of Lukumí

by Oracle Hekataios

Santeria, also known as Regla de Ocha ("Rule of the Orisha") and Lukum ("We are friends"), is an Afro-Cuban religious practice. Lukumí is based on Yoruba African religious practices and beliefs which were transferred to the Caribbean via the slave trade, particularly Cuba.[1] Cuba, and the Caribbean as a whole, received the second largest import of African slaves, all from diverse areas (although it did receive twice the amount of slaves than the United States). It is estimated that somewhere between 500,000 to 700,000 African slaves were brought to the island, most during the nineteenth century.

History

In modern-day Nigeria is located the Yoruba, a confederation of peoples who occupy the southwestern part of that country and are one of the three largest ethnic groups there.[2] Some are scattered throughout Benin and northern Togo, both west of Nigeria. At the turn of the millennium, there were a reported 20 million Yoruba. Traditionally among the most productive and

---

1 'Santeria': La Regla de Ocha-Ifa and Lukumi

2 Gorlinski

skilled craftspeople of Africa, many have farms, trade, or continue their crafts.

As a confederation, they have historically never been a single political unit. Rather, they have a shared culture and language. In pre-colonial times (i.e., prior to colonization by European powers in the nineteenth century), the Yoruba created independent political kingdoms and became the most urban of the ethnic groups within Africa. Each kingdom had at its center a capital where the seat of the Oba, or king, ruled. Eventually, the capitals—densely populated—grew into what are the modern-day cities of Oyo, Ile-Ife, Ibadan, Ilorin, and more. The largest of the Yoruba kingdoms became Oyo, while the religious center became Ile-Ife. The palaces of the Oba (or Alafin in the case of Oyo) were in the very center of the capital. While today many Yoruba are largely Christian or Muslim, syncretism still survives, and their religious beliefs and practices have seen an acute revival.

Beliefs and Practices

The deities (some say spirits) within the divine spectrum of the Yoruba's cultural and religious constellation of worship are the Orishas. But just what are the Orishas? Most scholars use the works of John Mason, a *babalorisha* ("father of the Orisha"), whose work covers vast territory of Yoruba culture and religion.[3] A *babalorisha* is a male priest, whereas an *iyalorisha* ("mother of the Orisha") describes a female priestess.

Mason breaks down the Lukumí/Yoruba word *orisha* into two separate ones: *orí* (head or consciousness) and *sà* (reflection or selection). This breaks down the inherent meaning within a specific, initiatory ceremony wherein there is a guiding Orisha who is the "selected head" of the individual undergoing the ceremony. This also reflects the belief concerning the relationship of Orisha with the head god, Olódumare.

3 Lele

Olódumare is the head of this divine spectrum. The Yoruba and their Afro-Diasporic descendants are a diffused monotheism, meaning it is not a monotheism with a one-sided focal lens on one deity at the expense of beliefs in other spirits or deities. Rather, it makes room for a divine spectrum of beings that are reflections, extensions, and/or representatives of the transcendent, Supreme God: Olódumare. The term "diffused monotheism" was coined by the Reverend E. Bolaji Idowu, a professor at the University of Ibaden in Nigeria, as well as pastor of Methodist Church Nigeria from 1974–1984.[4] He wrote the most important book on Yoruba theology: *Olódumare: God in Yoruba Belief.*

Other than the supremacy of Olódumare, there is also the concept of *ashé,* or life force/power. *Ashé,* according to Yoruba and Lukumí belief, is the very energetic foundation and sustainment of the cosmos. It lives in everything: the stars, the planets, the animals, the land with its stones and flora, as well as humans. It is the very bedrock of the relationship between the olorisha (initiate) and the Orisha. The cosmos and its very start came from Olódumare and their *ashé.*[5]

The practices of Lukumí/Yoruba include worship, offerings, and divination. Worship involves consistent performances of adoration on the feast days of the Orisha, as well as a personal development of insight and revelation on the part of the olorisha by giving offerings of food, money, and/or prayers. The start of the *mojuba* (prayers) always begins with the recitation of the *eggun* (ancestors and blessed dead). *Mojuba* is a compound word: *mo júbà* ("I pay homage to").

Offerings, or *ebbos,* are often at the very heart of the relationship and reciprocity of the Orisha and the olorisha. *Ebbos* are a central feature of the religion, from giving gifts to the *eggun,* to the Orishas themselves. There are a variety of *ebbos:*

---

4 Fiske, 10

5 I use "their" because Olódumare is beyond the concept of the sex and gender binary.

1. Votive, wherein simple things such as candles and incense are the gifts brought.
2. Food, with specific dishes cooked in specific ways to appease the Orishas.
3. Songs, with specific words and meters calling the Orisha.
4. Drumming, with specific meters beaten to worship and cause possession.
5. Animals, which are the most controversial of the practices to *aleyos* (strangers).

The largest concentration of *ebbos* is made up of the first four. So much creativity can go into them. What, then, is the purpose behind animal sacrifice? I'll get to that much later.

As stated in number four, another misunderstanding is possession. This is where an Orisha takes the body of the worshiper and makes movements, steps, and dances indicating which Orisha has a hold on them. It is a beautiful experience.

Divination involves two systems: *obi,* or the divination with a coconut; and the *diloggún,* or the use of cowrie shells. There is another branch of Lukumí known as Ifa wherein *babalawos* (fathers of the secrets) employ a variety of methods. The entire purpose of both branches is to hear the voice of the Orisha and ascertain direction for both olorishas and *aleyos* alike.

Age of the Empire

The Yoruba Empire, also known as the Oyo Empire, lasted for several hundred years. Its apex was between 1650–1750 CE.[6] Linguistic evidence suggests that two waves of peoples came into the region between 700 CE and 1000 CE. According to mythology, the founder was one Oduduwa, who migrated to the city of Ile-Ife. His grandson became the first Alafin (owner of the palace; a ruler), one of seven grandsons of Oduduwa who became the bringers and teachers of

6 Lotha

what would be the Yoruba Civilization via the area of Oyo. Due to its geographical position, it soon became a magnet of industry, trade, and coveted natural resources.

By the end of the sixteenth century, Oyo began to rise against its conquerors from the north—the Borgu and the Nupe. In the eighteenth century, Oyo conquered its neighbor, the Dahomey Kingdom. The Dahomey became a vassal state under Oyo rule, giving them tribute from the 1730s until 1819. Unlike the Yoruba, Dahomey had elite female warriors that were also spies. These female warriors, the Ahosi, were known for their fierceness in battle, superb skills, and capturing of other tribes for the Trans-Atlantic Slave Trade until its erasure, starting in the 1850s, from European colonial powers.[7]

The decline of the Oyo Empire began when the Alafin had internal disputes with his council of Obas, as well as loss of trade routes to colonial powers, revolts, and an unstable economy. Eventually, the Fulani—Africans who were among the first to convert to Islam—conquered the Oyo Empire in 1800. Incidentally, Islam was also a rising religious component among the Yoruba, having had contact with Islamic traders for five centuries.[8]

Birth of the Lukumí

As early as 1501, traders brought the Yoruba slaves to the Spanish and Portuguese colonies of the New World. In 1568, to answer the growing need for cheap labor, Cuba began to receive them as well. As the island's economy grew, cheaper labor was needed for the vast sugar and coffee plantations there. At first a meager number, the population of Yoruba slaves grew substantially. After the fall of the Oyo Empire, a continuous supply of slaves was brought to the New World.

Among the slaves were Yoruban priests and priestesses of various Orishas. Eventually, those who survived the grueling journey

---

7 Araujo

8 Busari, 44-66

were placed in Cabildos Negros (Houses of the Blacks).[9] After the ban of the Trans-Atlantic Slave Trade in 1821, some 800,000 more slaves were forcefully taken to Cuba as contraband until 1860. All were housed within the *cabildos.*

Here, slaves started to syncretize their Orishas with certain Catholic Saints (although syncretization had begun in Yoruba land, in the New World it grew a definitive character). Intermarriage began between Indigenous survivors of European colonization and the African slaves. Afro-Cuban culture was born.

The reason the syncretic religion survived was because of the *cabildos,* which acted like Spanish guilds or fraternities which were organized by African slaves of the same ethnic group. Spanish religious and political authorities believed that by easing the tension between slaves and slave owners, the *cabildos* could also act as a source from which the African population could draw strength while keeping their songs, drumming, and *patakis* (parables and myths) alive. The *cabildos* were an approved way to keep slaves entertained, and the *cabildo* belonging to the Yoruba became known as the Lukumí. The *cabildos* continued until they started a rebellion against the Spanish Empire. This caused them to be closed and gave rise to the *casa templo* (house temple) and a subsequent period of persecution.

The Rise in Cuba

Afro-Cuban peoples were born from this amalgamation. Roman Catholicism, the only legal religion on the island of Cuba, syncretized with Yoruba Orisha and gave birth to many cultural and spiritual traditions that today live on in ceremonies within Lukumí practices. In the nineteenth century, two major movements further influenced the development of Lukumí. The first was that of the teachings of the Frenchman Allan Kardec, whose practices—becoming known as Spiritism—blended with the existing religion to influence it in a remarkable way. Spiritism is a philosophical and

9 Rodriguez

religious movement that was born in France and spread to some European nations (but really found its growth in Latin American territories) which resulted in mediumship practices. Things such as reincarnation, the ever-presence of disembodied spirits which influence the living for good or for ill, and ancestral veneration via specific placements of an altar and other items really impacted the religion.

The second was the influx of Chinese indentured servants. The Chinese (nearly all men) brought ancestral Chinese religious figures and philosophies such as Buddhism, Confucianism, and Daoism. These later became syncretized with the Saints/Orishas. For example, Guan Gong, or the Cuban San Fang Kong, became associated with the Orisha Shango (a warrior-king), and was seen as an aspect of Saint Barbara (also syncretized with Shango). The Chinese immigrants intermarried with Afro-Cuban women.[10] Their artistry spread to the Afro-Cuban community and has today come to birth various designs. Such was the impact that Havana's Chinatown, El Barrio Chino de la Habana, is the oldest in Latin America and frequently draws tourists.

The Cuban Revolution

Orunile (Heaven is Home) perfectly encapsulates the notion that the land of your birth is Heaven, and that to carry the essence of your spirit is to be in the world, which is compared to a marketplace of sorts: a place of transactions of ideas, goods, services, and a notion of self.[11] What does this mean? It means that we have a destiny under the auspices of Olódumare, and that we come to Orisha to discover the best way to navigate this marketplace of life with their blessings on our health and other situations.

Lukumí began to spread over the island as whites also began to seek initiation into the Mysteries due to the accuracy of prophecy

10 Tsang

11 Otero

and the impact of healing that many received at the hands of the olorishas. Doctors were expensive, and even those with money often found their way to the olorishas because they would be given little to no hope in their diagnoses. Soon, this oral tradition began to be codified further thanks to olorishas. Many were illiterate, but those that were literate took out slips of paper and scribbled notes, thus further preserving the transmissions. These papers became known as *libretas de santos* (books of the saints). They were created due to the Lukumí priesthood's emphasis on *"Usted miga, oiga y calle"* (You look, listen, and stay quiet!). These books began to circulate among initiates around the turn of the nineteenth century.[12] They are a treasure trove of information containing spells, rituals, and divination methods.

From the nineteenth to the early decades of the twentieth century, prejudice has caused the religion to remain underground for fear of persecution. During the first half of the twentieth century, many religious practitioners were arrested, accused of *brujeria* (witchcraft). Religious items and notes were taken by the government and either destroyed or housed in the University of Havana's museum. Xenophobia also was rampant throughout the island against the Afro-Cuban population.

In 1959, the Cuban Revolution, initially led by the brothers Fidel and Raúl Castro, occurred. It was a reaction against the dictatorship of Fulgencio Batista who, in 1952, overthrew the democratic nation.[13] In many sectors of the island, Cubans were disappointed and angered against the eventual consolidation of power, the press, and the shambles of the economy caused by the Marxist-Lenin philosophy. This led to the great Cuban Exodus. As a direct result of the Exodus, many Cubans settled in parts of Florida and New York.

However, an amalgamation of influences worked to develop the Lukumí religion in the United States. One of the most historic milestones was when African Americans started being initiated. The

---

12 Miguel

13 Bustamante

first one was a man named Walter Eugene King. Born in 1928, King left the Baptist church of his youth and began studying African faiths and their various cultures, including Voudon in Haiti. Just before the Cuban Revolution in 1959, King traveled there to be initiated into the Mysteries of Lukumí.

As an omo-Obatala (child of the Orisha Obatala), he was given the religious moniker Efuntola Oseijeman Adefunmi.[14] Fusing his African studies with the religion, he established an Order, a temple, and, much later, a theological seminary. Although he later broke with Lukumí due to his disagreements with Cuban olorishas and traveled to Nigeria to be initiated by the Yoruba in Ile Ife, nonetheless his impact has been felt throughout the decades.

My Journey

Growing up, my mother was a *santera* (priestess) initiated to Yemaya. In Catholicism, Yemaya is syncretized with Our Lady of Regla (rule). Yemaya is the Orisha of the oceans and is perhaps one of the more popular of the Orishas. A large icon of the Orisha was in our closet, surrounded by *soperas* (soup tureens) filled with symbols and sacred items of various Orishas. This was my initial exposure. My mother's *madrina* (godmother in the faith) was also a skilled *espiritista* (practitioner of Espiritismo, the Spiritist branch of Lukumí). She held *misas* (seances) and read with tarot cards, coffee grinds, and knew how to do *limpias* (ritual cleansings) for people to be healed.

Much later, after a long and sordid history with Christianity, I learned that I felt drawn to the religion. However, I remember the obligations and taboos associated with it. It was also an overwhelming responsibility, and the rituals reminded me closely of the Pentecostal church I grew up in. I could not belong to anything so legalistic. Therefore, I did not seek anything, but instead turned towards my own Neopagan and polytheistic practices dedicated to Hekate and Dionysos. From being a solitary practitioner for quite some time, I

14 *The History of Oyotunji African Village*

later was able to become initiated into several Witchcraft Traditions. I also found myself maturing, leading covens, and actively teaching.

As a seer practicing my own brand of trance possession with deities, I later did professional readings at a nearby occult shop where I suddenly found myself practicing mediumship with the dead. This had me contact my own ancestors; it was later confirmed that the visions I had seen about them were true: I came from a line of *curanderas* (Mexican folk healers) from my biological father's side. I also learned that my eldest sister on my biological father's side was initiated to Oya, the Orisha of storms, whirlwinds, and the cemetery. The individual who oversaw the occult shop was also an *aborisha* (non-initiated devotee) of Lukumí.

The signs were all too clear: I needed the Orisha in my life. Looking for my own path, I decided to reach out to a former dedicant in one of my Witchcraft Traditions with whom I was still friends. It turned out that they were an Oba of a specific Ile located two hours north of me. I was determined that this was for me. This path I was dipping my toes in to figure out and ask questions was something not to be taken lightly. I knew how serious vows were, and I wanted to take my time. Lo and behold, another individual with whom I was acquainted with via witchcraft was also a part of the Ile! This was becoming too much. I asked them about their journeys.

I came to realize something in asking them about their own paths: I was hungry. Hungry for spirits to aid me in my health, in my finances, and in my life. I had a lot of traumas from growing up, as well as from a traumatic brain injury I sustained in 2012. I was lost too many times despite getting better spiritually and improving both physically and mentally. There was still a hole in my heart, and my ancestors were calling me to walk the road they prepared for me before I was ever born. Or was it my dream to walk that road which I was fulfilling at last?

I began as an *aleyo*, visiting once per month and finding a *padrino* (spiritual godfather) in the Ile who became my mentor. I watched ceremonies, which included working a lot, such as carrying buckets of water, digging holes, holding animals, and cleaning up messes.

Animal sacrifice, despite its reputation with the religion, is only less than 5% of the religion. The other 95% has to do with maturing one's attitudes and behaviors with ethics, values, and virtues, and in developing a devotional path with the Orishas. Animal sacrifice was only used in certain rites which called for strong *ashé* to be dispensed for initiations, "birthing" Orishas (that is, the handing down of the *soperas* with their sacred items that are given "life" via blood), and for ritual cleansings. Nothing went to waste. Except in cases where hexes needed to be lifted and cleansing was important, the animals were later cooked, and the community gathered in communal eating with gratitude to the animals giving their life for everyone.

In my own walk, I went from an *aleyo* to becoming an *aborisha* in 2023 when the Orisha named Obatala claimed me as his own. Obatala is known as the King of the White Cloth, the creator of humanity, and the ruler of the Orishas. He is depicted, usually, as an elderly man with a staff, dressed in white from head to toe. I then received my own stone with the essence of the Orisha Eleggua. Eleggua is the trickster, the master of the crossroads, and the one to whom *mojubas* and *ebbos* are done to first, opening the gates and carrying the prayers directly to the Orishas. Eleggua is first in everything. *Maferefun* (praise) *Eleggua!*

I realized the journey was becoming more serious the more ceremonies I attended. In addition, I was starting to become familiar with *misas,* where my *padrino,* Oba, and other future godsiblings channeled spirits and the dead to read me and determine my spiritual court. The court of an individual consists of one main spirit who helps lead the other spirits which surround the individual. These spirits may be blood ancestors or other types of characters such as gypsies,[15] Arabs, Indigenous peoples, or others. For me, my main spirit is an elevated individual who is named publicly as Mary of

15 I realize gypsy is a pejorative term for many, however, it is a term still used by many within Latin America to talk about certain spirits embodying or being from those people.

Sicily. According to the readings, she was a Sicilian with mixed Arab, Indigenous Sicilian, and North African blood. She was a powerful healer and occultist. Her mission is to teach me so she can ascend to the light herself.

As I continued my studies with books and practices, I came to understand one thing: Orishas are love, faithfulness, passion, beauty, and fulfillment. They are not at all the scary, primal beings I thought about and had heard about from *aleyos*. They are the very essence of nature; the spirits which move about, and, with their help, we walk the path destined for us sustained with love, power, and *ashé*.

I had to prove to myself that I could make myself, my *padrino*, and my Ile proud. I wanted to go further than merely being an *aborisha*. I wanted to be initiated into the Mysteries and join Obatala in becoming something more than myself. I wanted health, prosperity, and to know what awaited me as I continued.

So, in 2024, I went through the ordeals necessary to pass and became an *iyawo* (bride) of Obatala. I am now in the stages of my *iyaworaje*, which I will walk for a year and seven days. I wear all white, wear my *elekes* (sacred necklaces representing some Orisha), and practice devotions. I do the *work*. This religion is all about working hard to achieve your visions. I walk knowing I am watched carefully by the Orishas, as well as by my community. I continue to practice my other Traditions and call myself what my Oba does: a crowned witch. The Orisha live, and my life continues to be altered in beneficial ways. Each day, my Warriors (certain Orisha who protect the initiate) guide my path. Obatala speaks with me and through me. I am empowered, channeling their *ashé*. *Maferefun Obatala! Hekua Baba!* I am your child. May the blessings always continue.

Bibliography

Araujo, Ana Lucia. *Humans in Shackles: An Atlantic History of Slavery.* Chicago of University Press, 2024.

Busari, Muhummad Jamiu. "Islam in Yorubaland, Southwest Nigeria: A Historical Review of its Advent and Impacts till Present Time." *Al-Qanatir: International Journal of Islamic Studies,* vol. 33, no. 1, 2024.

Bustamante, Michael J. "The Cuban Revolution." *Oxford Research Encyclopedia of American History,* 2019, https://oxfordre.com/american history/display/10.1093/acrefore/9780199329175.001.0001/acrefore-9780199329175-e-643. Accessed 24 Sept. 2024.

Fiske, Edward B. "African Christians are Developing their own Theologies." *New York Times,* 12 Mar. 1971, pp. 10.

Gorlinksi, Virgina. "The Yoruba People." *Brittanica,* 2024, https://www.britannica.com/topic/Yoruba. Accessed 23 Sept. 2024.

Lele, Ocha'ni. *Osogbo: Speaking to the Spirits of Misfortune.* Destiny Books, 2014.

Lotha, Gloria. "Oyo Empire: Historical Kingdom in Western Africa." *Brittanica,* 2023, https://www.britannica.com/place/Oyo-empire. Accessed 23 Sept. 2024.

Miguel, Ramos W. *Obi Agbon: Lukumi Divination with Coconut.* Eleda.org Publications, 2012.

Otero, Solimar. *Afro-Cuban Diasporas in the New World.* University of Rochester Press, 2010.

Rodriguez, Omar. "Afro-Cuban Religion and Syncretism with the Catholic Religion." *Religion,* 2001, https://scholar.library.miami.edu/emancipation/religion1.htm. Accessed 23 Sept. 2024.

"'Santeria': La Regla de Ocha-Ifa and Lukumi." *The Pluralism Project: Harvard University,* 2025, https://pluralism.org/%E2%80%9Csanter%C3%ADa%E2%80%9D-the-lucumi-way. Accessed 19 Sept. 2024.

"The History of Oyotunji African Village." *Oyotunji,* https://web.archive.org/web/20160822080620/http://www.oyotunji.org/history.html. Accessed 24 Sept. 2024.

Tsang, Martin. *Chinese Influences on Life and Religion in Cuba.* Cuba and the Caribbean, 2023, https://cuba.miami.edu/people/chinese-influences-on-life-and-religion-in-cuba/index.html. Accessed 24 Sept. 2024.

Macumba and the Black Atlantic Tradition

by Nicholaj de Mattos Frisvold

Macumba is a perfect word to define Brazilian Sorcery and Witchcraft, given the myriad of interpretations and meanings this word has and especially how it became, in the twentieth century, used derogatorily in reference to black magic and "illicit magical practices." It was perceived as something different from Candomblé, which developed more formal structures and over time distanced themselves from the pragmatic chaos attached to the idea of Macumba. By the nineteenth century, "Macumba" began appearing in police records and newspapers, often used by the authorities to describe secret religious gatherings of African descendants in Rio de Janeiro. In doing this, police and governmental institutions like the Service for Orthophrenic and Mental Hygiene, which was established in 1934, were given the responsibility to make registries of *terreiros* and the practitioners of Afro-derived fringe religions, such as Candomblé and Macumba.[1] To be labelled insane came with some stigma, so many chose to avoid the registry and others sought ways of making African faiths an accepted religion.

In this same period, Candomblé, especially in Salvador, Bahia, objected to this term and distanced itself from being associated

---

1 *Terreiro* is a common name given to the temples of Macumba, as well as *tenda* (tent), *cabana* (shack), and *casa* (house).

with Macumba. In the nineteenth and early twentieth centuries, "Macumba" was used by outsiders (especially white elites and Catholic authorities) to describe all Afro-Brazilian spiritual practices, including Candomblé, Umbanda, and Quimbanda. But Candomblé took the measure of being recognised as an organised religion. Hence, even if *terreiro* is still used as a vernacular in reference to houses of Candomblé, the preferred term is Casa de Axé, or Ilé (house in Yoruba), which are of African, more specifically Yoruba, denomination. With urbanisation and modernisation, Candomblé turned themselves into a religion, different from Macumba, that became a catch-all term for Afro-Brazilian faiths, especially those associated with "low Spiritism" as a nomenclature for what was unruly, dangerous, loud, sorcerous, and savage. "Low Spiritism" was also equalled to *feitiçaria,* or sorcery. Hence, we find here a classification given to phenomena by Spiritists that perceived entities and souls of African or more humble origins as uninteresting, if not dangerous, and thus not welcome at the table. These spirits were *cabolcos, pretos velhos, Exus,* and *Pomba Giras,* spirits associated with the human struggle, the woods, and bohemia because Macumba is a living cult with very active and present entities that take an interest in the present.

Macumba evolved from Afro-Brazilian folk magic, which was practised mainly in Rio de Janeiro and São Paulo in the early 1900s. Today, Macumba consists predominantly of Umbanda, Quimbanda, and Jurema. Macumba is a term used to describe any African-derived spiritual practice in Brazil, often carrying connotations of witchcraft or sorcery. Over time, it became a popularised way to refer to certain forms of magic or ritual that involve working with spiritual forces to affect change in the world, be it for healing, protection, or harm. Hence, Macumba is an umbrella term for the plurality of Brazilian magic and spirituality, especially in relation to sorcery, or *feitiçaria.* This essay starts by presenting the early influences on Brazilian magic through the African, Native, European, and Catholic influences, weaving a web of intricate power and paradox. Presenting this canvas, Macumba is painted with the colours of beautiful, disorderly chaos in order to show how Macumba took shape from *santidade* in the fifteenth century, through the *calundus* and its rich spiritual and magical legacy and traditions, up to the many expressions of Macumba today. Brazil has always been a land that transforms through contrasts and by the power of transmutation, and so we find that cults and traditions as disparate as Umbanda, Jurema, Tambor de Mina, Catimbó, Encantaria, Quimbanda, and Candomblé are expressions of shared roots that have been taken into unique directions, presenting the rich tapestry of magic and spirituality in Brazil.

Let us have a look at the core of Macumba and its main content before looking at its predecessor, namely the *calundus*, and in this, presenting three historical practitioners that prefigured Macumba, namely Domingos Álvares, Luzia Pinta, and Juca Rosa.

At the Core of Macumba

In disclosing the core of Macumba, it is both helpful and interesting to look at two publications from the 1970s. One of these books was written by a French poet and essayist, and the other by French philosopher and a Brazilian sociologist. The first one is Serge Bramly, who published *Macumba* in 1975. Bramly writes about the countless centres (*terreiros*) of Macumba he encounters in Rio de Janeiro and paints a vivid image of a city filled with magic and spirits that overflow into streets and beaches. In this book, "Macumba" is used in reference to Umbanda, Xangô, Catimbó, Candomblé, Candomblé of Caboclo, and Pajelança. As a friend of Bramly, who was an Umbandist, told him:

> *Macumba is a general term. Originally, it meant the place where the black slaves performed their rites. Today, particularly in the state of Rio, it is used to designate all the different Afro-Brazilian sects. The black slaves who introduced the cult to Brazil were from many different areas up and down the eastern coast of Africa. There were Dahomians, Congolese, Fons, Angolans, and Geges... With time all these cults have more or less grown into one... Then there is Quimbanda, black magic....*[2]

2 Bramly 5–6

Looking at Marco Aurélio Luz and Georges Lapassade's book, *O Segredo da Macumba* (*Secrets of Macumba*), published in 1972, they write that Macumba has no connection whatsoever with Umbanda and is first and foremost the percussion instrument (a type of reco-reco), which would then give attention to Macumba as designated by its musicality and loudness. It is also worth taking notice that the sound of this instrument reminds one of the song of a bird known as *Rei Congo* (King Congo/*Psarocolius decumanus*), which brings attention to the importance of Congolese influences on Afro-Brazilian magic and sorcery in ways deliberate or more magical and unintended. They continue, stating that Macumba is a word derived from *mucambos,* which was an alternative name given to Quilombos, or Black settlements in colonial times. They conclude that Macumba represents the art, memory, and magic of the *pretos velhos,* the old Blacks.[3] In this way, Macumba, and especially Quimbanda, tells the story of restriction and emancipation; as they write, "Exu-Mangueira in Umbanda is servitude, but in Quimbanda, he is freedom."[4] They add that Macumba should be seen more as a lifestyle than a religion, that, despite having its roots and birth in Africa and then spread through the *favelas* of Rio de Janeiro, managed to embrace all social classes and colours in its aspiration towards freedom.[5]

The 1970s was indeed an extraordinary phase for Macumba. Through the activities of the medium Cacilda de Assis via her spirit guide, Seu Sete Rei da Lira (Exu, King of the Lyre), spectacles generated in the streets that attracted thousands of people celebrating Exu and the entities associated with "low Spiritism" in joyous and accepting ways. Guidance and healing followed, and these spectacles attracted poets, intellectuals, and musicians; hence, the perception of Macumba being a lifestyle related to music, samba, and spectacle, at least in Rio de Janeiro, was very much understandable.

---

3 Luz and Lapassade xxv

4 Ibid. xxvi

5 Ibid. 4–5

In the 1970s, Macumba was a multifaceted practice composed of African customs, memories, and traditions blended with Indigenous and Catholic influences under the banner of low Spiritism and *feitiçaria*. A Macumba altar made room for Catholic saints, like St. George, St. Lazarus, the Virgin Mary, and Jesus Christ, who also represented *orixás:* St. George was Ogum; St. Lazarus, Omolu; Virgin Mary, Iemanjá; and Jesus, Oxalá. Together with the saints, there were images of *caboclos*, or Indigenous spirits, and the *pretos velhos. Exus* were gathered around the *pretos velhos* and given canes, like the *pretos velhos*' tridents, tobacco (as they would to the Devil), *cachaça*, wine, coffee, and incense. In the sessions of Macumba *gira*, the medium would turn into the other, and this could include being possessed by a *caboclo*, like Cobra Coral, then an *Exu*, and then a *preto velho*... depending on the celebration.[6] The macumbeiro Waldemar Bento, in his 1939 book, *A Magia no Brasil* (*The Magic of Brazil*), presents the same landscape as Bramly, Luz, and Lapassade, but introduces both liturgy and philosophy to his description of Macumba. Exu and Pomba Gira, along with St. Michael the Archangel, as the owners of Quimbanda, are given supreme importance for the efficacy of Macumba. Laura de Mello e Souza observes in terms of the trajectory and metamorphoses of sorcery (*feitiço*) in Brazil:

> *The nature of sorcery thus mimicked the process of colonization: first, it was defined according to preexisting beliefs of the European colonizers whose systematic presence began in 1549, mainly along the coast. It then began to show the influence of autochthonous practice, some with a certain degree of syncretism.*[7]

In the case of Macumba and its African heritage, it is quite interesting to see how the African devotee of Sakpata, in its Brazilian

---

6 Ibid. 9

7 *Sorcery in Brazil: History and Historiography* 41

rendering as Saint Death in Quimbanda and a *preto velho* in Umbanda, takes on a creolised form which is so very Brazilian and speaks the language of Macumba in all colours and volumes.

Luzia Pinta and the Calundus

The word *calundus* was used in Brazil as early as the seventeenth century. It appears in colonial records and writings describing African and Afro-Brazilian spiritual and healing practices. One of the earliest references comes from Father Jorge Benci's work *O Soldado Prático*, where he describes *calundus* as ritualistic dances, trances, and invocations of spirits among enslaved Africans, involving spirit possession and healing, often associated with Kongo and Bantu traditions. By the eighteenth century, documents from the Portuguese Inquisition mentioned *calundus* in cases against enslaved people accused of practising *feitiçaria.* Several of the elements of *calundus* we find today in Macumba.

Luzia Pinta is perhaps the one who exemplifies the *calunduseiro* better than anyone. Luzia Pinta was born in Luanda, Angola, already a slave in her homeland, and was brought to Brazil. Mello e Souza imparts how she, in 1739, was accused of the practice of *feitiçaria,* and stood trial in Lisbon in front of the Inquisition. On 12 August 1743, she was subject to torture. Before that, she was brought to Brazil in 1710, to the city of Sabará in Minas Gerais, where she eventually gained her freedom. Her *calundus* was described as being conducted with her dressed "as an angel" or as a "Turkish person" on a throne. She held an axe and a sword, directing the movements around a shrine made from diverse types of fabrics. She would direct the ritual and its rhythm, administrating drinks that led to vomiting and divinatory ecstasy in rituals of healing. She was assisted by two other women, also from Angola, and one male slave from another district in the performance of these rituals. Luzia Pinta said to the Inquisition that she was performing the rituals she was taught in Angola after she, at the age of twelve, fell into cataleptic trances and had visions, similar to Joan of Arc and Teresa of Avila. She insisted that there was nothing of the Devil in what she was doing. The fact that she was screaming out for the aid of St. Anthony during her torture might indicate that she truly saw herself as working within the Congolese Christianity she knew and practiced. The final verdict of the Inquisition was inconclusive, but since she was under suspicion of being a *feitiçeira*, she was sent in exile to Algarve, where the traces of her dissipate into the fog of history.

Luzia Pinta commonly gathered a small contingent of her enslaved countrymen to aid in her rituals. Two Angolan women sang, and a man played an *atabaque* (small drum) in order to stir the "winds of divination." As the volume of the music rose, Luzia's ancestors ascended into her head, causing her to jump around "like a goat." Upon entering a trancelike state, Luzia continued to be racked with "great tremors." Dressed in ritual garb that included ribbons in her hair, rattles around her wrists and ankles, and a dagger in her hand, Luzia offered remedies for people's illnesses.

As the cult of *calundus* spread out from Bahia and travelled in all directions, we encounter references to *calundus* in 1730, particularly in the northeast of Brazil, that were called *jurema.* It spread rapidly through communities of more Indigenous orientation in Pernambuco and Paraiba, making its way south of Recife by the middle of the eighteenth century. The rituals of *jurema* were of a healing nature, and the rituals combined dancing and singing with the ingestion of a hallucinogenic drink made from the roots of the Jurema tree (*Mimosa hostilis*) to facilitate contact with the invisible world and its masters and teaching spirits. As the healing cult spread, it came to include peoples of African and Portuguese ancestry, and the cult became more and more inclusive. The result of this new ethnic mixture was a transformation in ritual practice. For example, in 1781, members of the *jurema* cult in Una, near Serinhaém, integrated some Christian elements into their rituals;

one of them consisted of, prior to the consummation of *jurema*, consecrating the ritual beverage by dipping a crucifix into it.

All of this was popularly referred to as "Macumba," giving the idea that it was about any form of sorcerous heresy with an African scent. It was, however, through *calundus* and Macumba that Africa entered Brazil, and in this regard, Domingos Álvares is another interesting forerunner to Macumba and its African fragrance and sorcerous wisdom.

Domingos Álvares Represents the Iconic Macumbeiro

Domingos Álvares was born around 1710, in a Vodou community dedicated to the earth spirit Sakpata in the Mahi region of the modern-day West African nation of Benin, to spiritual leaders of the community, Afnaje and Oconon. King Agaja begins to view Álvares as a threat and orders Álvares to be captured and sold by Atlantic slave traders around 1729. Álvares is taken to sugar plantations in northeastern Brazil and continues his work as a healer. In 1742, Catholic authorities finally arrested Álvares and sent him to Lisbon, where the Portuguese Inquisition tried him for witchcraft. Although interrogators attempted to get Álvares to admit to entering into a pact with the Devil, he refused to admit this and explained in great detail the nature of his work during the two years of his investigation. Álvares insisted that he never departed from the tenets of Roman Catholicism, but the inquisitors refused to accept his explanations, and he was tortured on the rack. In 1744, he was forced to march to Lisbon's main public square and make a public confession, at which point he was punished by whipping and banished for life to Castro Marim, Portugal.

When Domingos came to Brazil, he was bought to work on sugar cane plantations, but he wanted to work as a healer and exercise his true profession as a priest of Sakpata. His resistance towards the hard labour on the plantation ended with him being suspected of poisoning his owner. Consequently, he was sold to a man in Rio de Janeiro who saw potential in him working as a healer there. Domingos was allowed to set up various centres for medicine and cults around Rio de Janeiro and his skill and charisma drew people fast and plenty. His practice was similar to Luzia Pinta, with trances and healing being done with the help of his *vodouns:* Sakpata (Obaluwaye), Gu (Ogum), Dan (Danbalah), and Hevioso (Sango), that was found under a lemon tree (*Citrus Limon*), which in Vodou is sacred to serpentine *vodouns* in general.[8]

The local priests were not too happy to see these *terreiros* of Vodoun being established side by side with their healing practice and raided these *terreiros.* But even like this, Domingos just relocated and replicated his success wherever he went until 1742. That year, he was sent to Lisbon to stand trial for the Inquisition, accused of making pacts with the Devil, which he refused to admit; on the contrary, he insisted that he was living according to the Roman Catholic faith and was a true believer. It is difficult to say in what ways he understood Catholic theology, but we know that he knew several prayers: Our Father, Ave Maria, the Oration of the Just Judge, and others. He attended mass and also engaged in confession, not under pressure but as a way of exploring the healing rituals of the Catholic *vodouns.* Eventually, he was sent to the tribunal in Évora.

From 1660–1760, Évora was the most prolific tribunal for the Inquisition in Iberia, partly why the witches from this region became renowned. It also comes from the famous witch known as Lagarrona, written about in the book *Historia das Antiguidades de Evora* by Amador Patrício, the pseudonym of Martim Cardoso de Azevedo, which was published in 1739. There is even a legend speaking of how she handed over her books on magic to the sorcerous Saint Cyprian in Babylon, hence forging a connection there with

8 In Marabout Sufism, the lemon tree is also considered a meeting point for djinn.

the tradition of Cyprian, and perhaps casting herself in the image of Justinia. The tribunal of Évora exiled Domingos to Castro Marim in the year 1749, and with his exile, he also disappeared from the eyes of history. Domingos can be said to represent a prime example of the Brazilian spiritualist or spirit worker, a person who sees power and spirit as they are and not through the filters of religion and the dogmas of various denominations. He focused on commonality more than differences. A Catholic priest was considered a spiritual peer and colleague, as revealed in words like *Avóduno* and *Vodunon,* which the Gbe-speaking people used in reference to Catholic and Vodoun priests. This similarity between priests of different cults being equal in status also ignited competition. For instance, when Domingos arrived in Recife, he was challenged not only by Catholic priests but, also two spirit workers already well established in the city: Antônia Maria, who was white, and Angolan Joana de Andrade. They all made up a part of the field of Macumba, depending on who was witnessing and judging the magic of the various practitioners.

Mandingas, Macumbas, and Reza Forte

The incorporation of Catholic elements amongst the Blacks and natives also went the other way, like in the case of Father Alberto de Santo Tomás, who spoke out loudly against the "negro sorcerers," and instead recommended using the Roman ritual for exorcism, fronting this as far more effective than the healing rituals of *calundus.* Not only that, but he also Africanized Catholicism by offering *bolsas de mandingo* and *patuás,* which were charms and talismans wrapped in cloth or leather, only with the addition of holy items, be it Bible verses, wax from consecrated candles, or other items that witches and heretics on the continent used in their sorcery making. Father Alberto introduced elements both from European witchcraft and African Macumba in his Catholic charms and talismans.

The Afro-Catholic hybridity of Macumba is well demonstrated in the magical artefact, the *bolsas de mandingo.* These were protective amulets of great repute that were composed of a variety of ingredients that, in combination, would create a specific occult power. The manufacturing of these talismans is remarkably similar in idea to what we find in Scandinavia when assembling the troll bag, and in the Pennsylvania Braucherei or Witchcraft with their Brauche Bag or "witch bag," although the Mandinka culture originated in the parts of Africa we today call Gambia, Senegal, and the Ivory Coast. One fascinating example we find of both content and the thinking behind these *mandingo* bags is in the case of José Francisco Pereira, a native of Ouidah, who was arrested in Lisbon on charges of witchcraft in 1730.[9]

Pereira was born in Africa, enslaved in Brazil, and eventually brought to Portugal, where he gained fame as one of the most prestigious *mandingeiros,* or *mandingo* practitioners. An essential part of these pouches was drawings, which in the following photos were made both in ink and blood, and represented a distinctly sorcerous African take on Catholic mysteries. On the left, we find a design that reminds us of a medallion of protection, the pouther borders decorated in ways typical for several West African cultures. In contrast, the design itself uses Christian lithography and symbolism in a demanding way, the arrows on the cross demonstrating the direction and insistence of the prayers in a way that fused African and Catholic iconography in a pragmatic spirit that made root for Pereira's magical and theological understanding of these elements. The other drawing to the right is richer in detail. Yet, the essential potency is in the crucified and resurrected Christ with the symbolism of crossed arrows he most likely was exposed to in Brazil by practitioners of Angolan and Congo descent, given how Jesus Christ in this phase of his mystical unfolding was considered

---

9 Rarey 20–33

a powerful *nkisi* able to perform incredible magic, and the motifs of sun, moon, arrows, skulls, hearts, and bones do make up a distinctly Congolese iconography.[10]

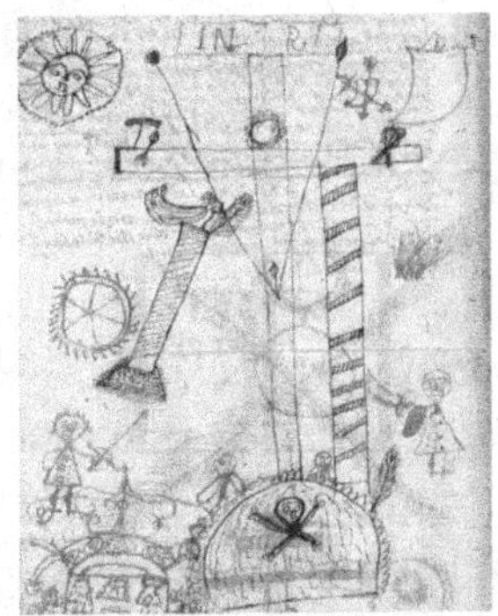

Let's pause here and gather the various pieces. Pereira was from Benin and was sold into slavery under the rulership of King Agaja (1708–40), and thus suffered the same fate as Domingos Álvares, which would suggest that Pereira and Álvares represented similar threats, which for Agaja was the Dahomeyan people with ties to the Oyo state in Nigeria and the cults of Sakpata and Sango. In 1728, Oyo's cavalry invaded Dahomey and King Agaja became subservient to Oyo rule until his death, which means that those who were sold into slavery by King Agaja in this period were sold because they were considered to be a threat to his hegemony, usually both by reputation of being skilled in sorcery as well as their ties to Oyo cults, especially Sakpata. This means that the culture he would have been familiar with would be Benin *vodouns* and Yoruba *orisas,* not the Mandinke *marabouts.* Parts of this knowledge must have been taught to Pereira in Brazil, where slaves from Central Africa and Congo dominated the Brazilian coastline from Recife in the northeast to Rio de Janeiro in the southeast.[11]

---

10 Thornton 147–167; Martínez-Ruiz

11 Sweet 61

Also, in the due process against him, it is stated that he was using *pedra d'ara* in all his bags, which most likely referred to the sacred slab of marble engraved with a cross where the chalice and *paten* are placed—but *pedra d'ara* is also the Portuguese name for *edun ara,* the thunderstone ascribed to Sango and Sakpata.... It is less important to verify what was spoken of in this case and more important to highlight the ambiguity of items and ideas that characterises Macumba, which suggests a transformative quality associated with all things, whether material or in the realm of ideas. That Pereira was deemed a *mandingueiro* instead of a macumbeiro was most likely because he focused on manufacturing charms and amulets more than the rituals of healing and sorcery associated with Macumba as a practice. Both *mandingas* and Macumba were, however, equivalent to *feitiçaria* and witchcraft, and the contents of Pereira's bags were revealed in the minimum "error," if not as heresy. In the bags were found gunpowder, bullets, flint, coins, human remains, animal remains, verses from scripture, and herbs that spoke of the "beliefs regarding the efficacy of transformative substances with seemingly supernatural powers."[12] The content in these bags also points towards a very pragmatic and diverse collection of *materia magica* that speak to a perception of similitude through difference, where a Bible verse speaking of divine protection is brought together with a bullet and herbs carrying the same virtue. A knowledge that for sure came from Africa but was modified by practitioners along the way wherever they met in the New World, taking up new elements, changing, becoming more affluent, yet still at the core remaining the same, a charm of protection. The name for *mandinga* bags was not necessarily made by a person from the Mande ethnic group, the name is more referring to the enormous influence of these people.

---

12 Martínez-Ruiz 74

The larger Mande ethnic group originates from the regions of Mali, Guinea, Senegal, Mali, Gambia, and the Ivory Coast. They constituted the Mali empire from the thirteenth to sixteenth century, which included people like Mansa Musa, reputedly the richest man in human history. The Mali Empire adopted Islam, but Berber traditions also influenced this Afro-Islamic culture with the school of Sufism known as Marabout, which became the title of Mandinka spiritual leaders and practitioners of magic (Marabout from the Arabic *murābiṭ*) who practice Sufi Islam but also blend in traditional African spiritual practices. Some were mystical scholars, but others were known for their propensity for sorcery and manufacturing amulets and charms (*bolsa de mandingas, patuá, gris-gris,* Brauche bag, and so forth). Beyond being enormously popular in colonised Africa, Iberia, and Brazil, most likely the *mandingos* and their reputation for dense sorcery through the activities of the Marabouts gave way to one of the earliest *Exus* in Quimbanda, Exu Marabô.

Mandingeiros were also associated with another Muslim group of ritual specialists, the Malê, which differentiated from the Mandinka by being Yoruba-speaking Muslims. Also, here we see the reputation for powerful sorcery-coloured Quimbanda, in this case, the line of Quimbanda called Malé or Malei, which also happens to be phonetically related to *mal* (bad/evil), generating phonetic and linguistic power to an entity like Exu Marabô. Allow me to describe this *Exus,* as this demonstrates the cultural and magical amalgam that Quimbanda is and how Exu embodies this versatility of magical cultures. First off, Exu Marabô is given a syncretism with daemons from *Grimorium Verum,* by the Umbandist, and by extension, macumbeiro, as Aluísio Fontenelle, in his book *Exu,* published in 1954. In this text, several *Exus* are given daemonic syncretisms, and Exu Marabô is equated with Put Satanakia, most likely Satanachia in the *Grand Grimoire,* just to escape the standard *Verum* reference, perhaps? Either way, these daemons are attributed to lust and seduction, and these qualities are also attributed to Macumba under Exu Marabô's jurisdiction. The description in *Exu* gives him French, Brazilian, and African attributes both from Congo and Sierra Leone:

> *This Exu is a great healer with a preference for fine wines and cigars. It is said that this Exu speaks and writes French fluently and is an all-round gentle and wise spirit of a more aristocratic bend. He is followed by a crow that protects him fiercely and especially Absinth, Chartreuse, port and red wine is to his liking. He dwells at the crossroads and in temples decorated to his glory. His pontos cantados refer to him as ganga, which reveals a deep connection with the Bantu faith and this suggests that this Exu is one of the older Exus. Some have suggested that his name means "the Exu who protects his people."*

But I find it likely that his name is derived from the Marabó of Ghana and Sierra Leone, a sorcerer, or *ganga*. It might also be that we find a connection here with the *sufi silsilya* known as Marabout, which has its larger spread in North and Northwestern Africa.

Marabô is also related to crossroads and takes a particular interest in errant people and pilgrims; hence, his domain in the kingdom is of the tracks. Given his old and wise stature, he is well-equipped to give good advice and possessions tend to be of a gentle and clearly articulated type—but this is, however, not always the case. There is a potential in almost all *Exus* to become enraged and uncontrollable, and so it is also with Exu Marabô. There are few or no curse words coming from him; he prefers to challenge people coming to him directly rather than using foul words. He is aristocratic in every sense and can often be perceived to have a hot effect on women, increasing their sexual senses and desires. It is not uncommon to apply this *Exu* in works for the restoration of male libido and potency.

Among the daemonic spirits of the northern hemisphere, his relation to Put Satanakia links this *Exu* to the realm of Solomonic Magic, in particular Armadel and Legemeton. His domain is largely that of occult inspiration and the giving of wisdom, especially concerning stellar mysteries and works of the crossroad and the crow. His sacred items include iron, castor seeds and oil, and any kind of quartz, especially those made yellow by sulphur, which is one of his sacred colours, along with red and black. He is depicted as a bald but bearded, dark-skinned deity of a heavy build. His red cape forms into wings around him. He is armed with a sword and chalice and guided by the crow.

One of his *pontos cantados* (sung points), or summoning songs, goes as follows, addressing that this *Exu* is associated with cyclops in the wood and that he is a *ganga,* a sorcerer from Congo:

Eu fui no mato gangá, apanhar cipó
I went to the woods, gangá, to get liana,
Eu vi um bicho gangá, de um olho só,
I saw a beast, ganga, with only one eye,
O Exu gangá, o Exu gangá é Marabô.
The Exu gangá, The Exu gangá is Marabô.

Juca Rosa and the Macumba Carioca

All of these influences find themselves being masterfully wielded by the famous "black sorcerer" José Sebastião da Rosa, better known as Juca Rosa.

Juca Rosa was reputed to manufacture breviaries, a type of *bolsa de mandinga,* also known as *patuá,* to break sorcery and protect against it.[13] He was one of the most important Black religious leaders in Rio de Janeiro. Born to an African mother in 1833, he was literate and served in the Army. He worked as a coachman and tailor before becoming the leader of a religious sect with many followers, where he was known as Pai Quimbombo, considered to have great supernatural power. He spent a few months in Bahia learning the mysteries of African religion. When he returned to Rio de Janeiro, he set up a very famous temple in the neighborhood of "Little Africa," where Black people from the North and Northeast of Brazil gathered.

The newspapers of the time called him a "black sorcerer." He was the subject of newspaper articles due to his involvement with prostitutes, seamstresses, poor and Black women, and white and

13 Trindade 94–99

married women from important families in the political life of Brazil's court. Most of his followers were women who were drawn to his attractiveness and penetrating gaze. He was always well-dressed and wore expensive jewelry. In addition to slaves and freed men and women, many important people were found to be present in his temple, such as politicians, merchants, members of the social elite, and intellectuals. He established relationships with important people in society, and his rituals and magical celebrations brought a great number of people to him. He was known for "provoking passions, taking away men's sexual potency, making them sick and succumbing to diseases."[14] All for money—wrote newspaper editors. Juca Rosa worked in a village located on Rua do Núncio, in front of a *congá* with religious images. In a dimly lit room, he performed voodoo rituals. He distributed amulets to wear around the neck. He embodied Pai Quimbombo. In his *terreiro*, he received important people, as well as beautiful ladies who he bewitched and who brought joy to Juca's life. An anonymous complaint, published in the "Diário de Notícias," addressed to the Court's second police chief, accused him of sexual involvement with several women. Juca Roca stopped his activities and was arrested and prosecuted for fraud. The incident became a hot topic for the press and was reported in newspapers in several Brazilian capitals.

According to the journal, the accuser was a 24-year-old man who met Juca when he sought treatment for a sore arm. He paid 30 thousand réis as an advance to buy medicine and participated in a ritual. He watched Juca perform a "binding," surrounded by "trinkets," barefoot and shirtless. The accuser then says he transformed enmity into affection, and he also advised how to overcome any daily difficulty. According to the newspaper article, "it was at this moment that all the attendees kissed his right hand and bowed their heads to the floor."[15] The trial began on January 5, 1871, but Juca had already been imprisoned for eight months. The room was

14 Ibid.

15 Ibid.

packed with authorities, important people, women, and followers, giving the Court a rather nonchalant and festive tone. His lawyer was Dr. Felipe Jansen de Castro Albuquerque, and according to "Diário de Notícias," the prosecution lawyers had to wage a "heroic struggle to extract the truth" from witnesses who were terrified by the look Juca was giving them, fearing malefic enchantments being sent towards them by the glance of the mighty sorcerer's eyes. The newspaper continued its campaign against Rosa by highlighting spells and murders that he had promoted and warning the authorities to continue the persecution of him and others of same ilk. Eventually, he was convicted, but not for his *mandingas* and Macumba, since the Imperial Criminal Code did not cover crimes of this type; instead, he was convicted of fraud and sentenced to six years of imprisonment.

The case of Juca Rosa is very intriguing as it demonstrates what happened when Macumba took a decisive urban turn. The practitioners of Macumba became actors of change and began to interact with all social classes. Juca Rosa served as an example for several movements that the elite intended to repress; it was Macumba, African people, or the subversives like prostitutes or artists in general from the walks of bohemia.

Some of the fundamental traces of the Macumba can already be discerned in Juca Rosa's descriptions of the rituals practised in the final years of the nineteenth century. The first thing that calls for attention in the descriptions of these rituals and practices is that the essential framework is really of Bantu or Congo origin: the pillar of Juca Rosa's work was possession by ancestral spirits, mainly by a spirit named Pai Quibombo (Father Quibombo/Tata Quibombo), meaning Father Okra, in reference to its phallic nature and association with semen as a quality of fire. We can see here already the first stages of what would become, in the Umbanda of the twentieth century, the important class of spirits named *pretos velhos*.

In the rituals, there would be music, dance, and a lot of food and drink. At a certain moment, Rosa would go into a trance, when, as it was said, he would receive spirits into his body, or "talk to the spirits," and then he was transformed into, or began to act as, Father Quibombo, and not as José Sebastião da Rosa. In this state of incorporation, he attended the people as Tata Quibombo, not as Juca.

The music of the meetings was usually played by four musicians, two of them playing a percussion instrument called a *macumba.* That important detail was the reason why Juca Rosa was also known in Rio de Janeiro as the "Chief of the Macumbas." That indicates that the name Macumba, which would become the popular denomination for this kind of magical work, was in origin an appellation given by outsiders of the cult due to the use of the musical instrument. We are also aware that Juca Rosa was not the only sorcerer to work like that in Rio de Janeiro at the time, but he was considered to be the most powerful.

The description of some of the ordered works made by Juca Rosa to his clients is also very telling. He used black and red clothes, offered up sacrificial items, and also made animal sacrifices. What we see from this little peak into the works of Juca Rosa reveals a very simple structure:

1. The *tata*/tutelary spirit of the Quimbandeiro is invited in to do the work or endow the vessel with the powers of his Tata.
2. Rhythm is used to attract the spirit; in this case the reco-reco and drums, and thus these sounds came to be associated with "Macumba" going on.
3. Spirit offerings, including blood sacrifice were performed.
4. Magic/healing/help was performed in this altered state of consciousness with a spirit tied to the practitioner's ancestors, be it by blood or spiritual descent.

A Bantu structure further invites in the importance of the woods, because the Bantu speaking people, the Kongo people were tied in to the mysteries of wood and plants, and hence we might suggest that when we speak of things "Bantu," we are speaking of what the Yorubas referred to as the realm of Osanyin, the Lord of the Woods, the doctor of spirits. This suggestion will be in harmony with the accounts of missionaries recounted by Arthur Ramos and Nina Rodrigues that emphasise how all the *ngiras* (ritual celebrations focused on spirit incorporation) of the macumbeiros were held in the woods, and how the practitioners were sent out in the woods to bring back their *tatas* and invite them to take possession of the medium.

Beyond *Exus,* the entities of Macumba are *caboclos,* and *pretos velhos,* which nowadays belong to Umbanda but make up part of Macumba. *Caboclos* preserve the memory of land, the voices that still reverberate in the wind that shape the leaves and trees and whisper through the blood that anointed and marked this land. *Pretos velhos* was and still is the memory of Guiné, or Africa. With their rosaries, pipes, and Portuguese names, they represent the gates of Janus and the Brazilian metamorphosis, where Brazil makes everything that enters its own child and legacy.

Macumba was made possible through the *pretos velhos,* the old Blacks, who were a sign and symbol of the Black legacy that became the fertile soil for Macumba. Preto Velho, in the form of Pai Antônio, was channelled through the young medium Zélio de Moraes, the founder of Umbanda since its inception in 1908, but the original were, of course, people like Domingos Álvares, José Francisco Pereira, Luzia Pinta, and Juca Rosa. And we might wonder why these fiery sorcerers are represented by old Blacks of a tranquil nature, which is due to the *pretos velhos* being associated with the line of souls or saints, also known as the African line presided over by Omolu or Soponna, that in Brazil was worked and understood to be under the icon of Saint Death, orbed in red, holding a chest of mysteries, perhaps the secret to his transformations or the abstruse dimensions of Macumba? Beyond being a mystery unto itself, this form is naturally due to all death associated with the Trans-Atlantic Slave Trade and its consequences, but in death, we find wisdom, and hence, history through death gives the form to the Preto Velho we know today.

The figure of the Preto Velho is one of the most profound and revered entities in Afro-Brazilian religious traditions, particularly in Umbanda and Candomblé de Caboclo. Representing the spirits of formerly enslaved African elders, *pretos velhos* are seen as guides, healers, and protectors, embodying wisdom, humility, and resilience. Their presence in spiritual practices reflects both historical memory and contemporary reverence for ancestral knowledge. Preto Velho, in its wise old form, emerges from Brazil's colonial history of slavery (1500s–1888), during which millions of Africans were forcibly brought to the country. Enslaved individuals maintained and adapted their spiritual practices despite repression, blending African, Indigenous, and Catholic traditions. Over time, the *pretos velhos* became a symbol of ancestral strength, as these spirits were believed to have endured suffering, yet have emerged with deep compassion and enlightenment. Unlike the more warrior-like spirits of the *caboclos* (Indigenous ancestors) or the spirits of the streets and more untamed domains, like *Exus,* the *pretos velhos* represent a calm, meditative presence. These spirits are often depicted as elderly men or women, dressed humbly, smoking a pipe, and offering wise counsel while drinking their coffee, usually sweetened, which becomes a cup holding the memory of colonisation and slavery. The pipe smoke itself carries symbolic significance, representing the transformation of suffering into wisdom and the communication between the physical and spiritual realms.

During spirit incorporations, the medium embodying Preto Velho may move slowly, bent over as if carrying the weight of history, and speak softly and deliberately. These performances are a form of sacred embodiment, allowing the wisdom of the ancestors to be transmitted to the community, along with the strength and kindness through suffering they show is possible. They represent a bridge between past suffering and present empowerment, an embodiment of ancestral resilience, collective memory, and the transformative power of wisdom.

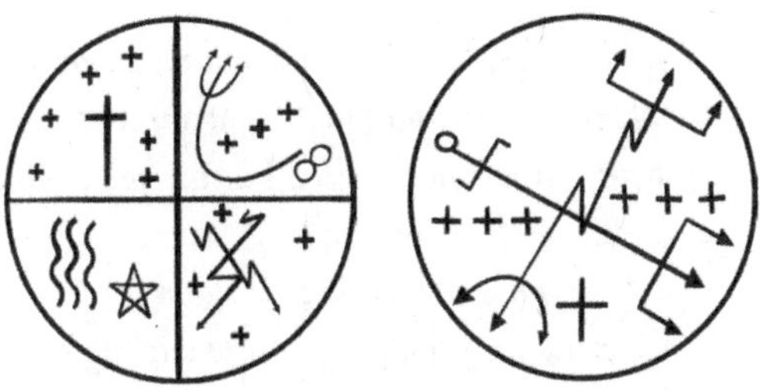

All these elements are engraved on the *ponto riscado* (spirit signature) of the *pretos velhos* as a collective. Here we see the connection with death and the rosary, with the watery grave, or *Kalunga,* along with the trident of Exu, and the lighting of Nzazi, the *nkisi* of thunder and sorcery, that also represents Nzambi, or "God." We see his connection to Quimbanda and healing through the trident and the triple crossroad, his affinity with water and crossings, the pentagram, which is the universal symbol for *pretos velhos,* and lastly, the crossed lightning that, amongst other symbolic values, has at its root the presence of Nzambi, the Bantu, and Congo idea of God. But this idea of the lightning crossing another stroke of lightning we also find in the *ponto riscado* of Exu Marabô (to the right). Subtle hints giving a nod to Exu, Preto Velho, and Nzambi are found everywhere in the vein of Macumba we know as Quimbanda. Let's summarise the legacy of Preto Velho as the blood of Macumba in poetic meters and allow that to be the end of this presentation.

From the embers of time, he rises,
feet bare upon the earth,
hands worn by toil, yet soft with healing.

Eyes like deep wells—dark, knowing, endless,
where sorrow and laughter walk together,
where chains once rattled but no longer sing.

He smokes his pipe slowly,
whispering prayers between the curling smoke,
words heavy with history are made light with love.
"Child," he says, voice like the roots of an ancient tree,
"there is no wound the earth cannot heal,
no sorrow that cannot become song."

Bent with age, yet towering in spirit,
he walks where the forgotten souls linger,
carrying the weight of yesterday
so that tomorrow may be free.

Pai Congo—you support the weary,
You heal wounds, seen and unseen,
With your prayers, rosary and pipe
The wisdom of ashes, the breath of memory
Saravá Pai!

Bibliography

Benci, Jorge. *O Soldado Prático.* 1678.

Bento, Waldemar L. *A Magia no Brasil.* Jornal do Brasil, 1939.

Bramly, Serge. *Macumba.* City Lights, 1994.

Fontenelle, Aluísio. *Exu.* 1954.

Frisvold, Nicholaj de Mattos. *Exu.* Scarlet Imprint, 2012.

Luz, Marco Aurélio and Georges Lapassade. *O Segredo da Macumba.* Paz e Terra, 1972.

Martínez-Ruiz, Bárbaro. *Kongo Graphic Writing and Other Narratives of the Sign.* Temple University Press, 2013.

Mello e Souza, Laura de. "Sorcery in Brazil: History and Historiography." *Sorcery in the Black Atlantic.* University of Chicago Press, 2011, pp. 41–54.

Molina, N. A. *Antigo Breviario de Rezas e Mandingas.* Editora Espiritualista, 1973.

Patrício, Amador. *Historia das Antiguidades de Evora.* 1739.

Querino, Manuel. *Costumes Africanos no Brasil.* Bibliotheca de Divulgação Scientifica, 1938.

Ramos, Arthur. *O Folk-Lore Negro do Brasil.* Civilização Brasileira, 1935.

Rarey, Matthew Francis. "Assemblage, Occlusion, and the Art of Survival in the Black Atlantic." *African Arts,* vol. 51, no. 4, 2018, pp. 20-33.

Rodrigues, Nina. *O Animismo Fetichista dos Negros Bahianos.* Civilização Brasileira, 1900.

Sweet, James H. *Domingos Álvares, African Healing, and the Intellectual History of the Atlantic World.* University of North Carolina Press, 2011.

Thornton, John K. "The Development of an African Catholic Church in the Kingdom of the Kongo, 1491–1750." *The Journal of African History,* vol. 25, no. 2, 1984, pp. 147–167.

Thornton John K. "The Kingdom of Kongo and Palo Mayombe: Reflections on African-American Religion." *Slavery & Abolition*, vol. 37, no. 1, 2016, pp. 1–22.

Trindade, Diamantino Fernandes. *Feiticeiros e Feitiçaria no Segundo Império do Brasil.* Editora Conhecimento, 2019.

Ptolemy's Book on the Benefits of Stones and Gems

by Rain Al-Alim

The Arabic occult literature contains various mineralogy treatises, known as lapidaries, which adapt a vast array of inherited written sources, preserving ancient traditions through translations from Greek, Indian, Hebrew, Persian, and Mesopotamian texts. They explore the magical properties and benefits of stones and gems, describe the engraving of talismanic figures or glyphs, and detail their construction at specific astrological times and their relations or correspondences to the heavenly bodies—planets and stars.

The focus of this article is on a particular apocryphal Arabic text titled *Kitāb al-Aḥjār,* by Pseudo-Ptolemy, which is a short lapidary work.[1] The treatise attributed to Ptolemy describes instructions for crafting various talismans from different stones and gems, specific talismanic images and glyphs that should be engraved on them, and the specific astrological times and conditions for their proper creation with an appendix on testing the precious stones.

---

1 Rovati

Two known copies of the text exist: one in the Vatican Library, MS Sbath 48 (19r–21v), likely from the thirteenth or fourteenth century with an unknown scribe, and another in the National Library of France, MS Arabe 2772 (39r–44v), dated to 1329 CE and copied by Muḥammad b. al-Mubārak b. 'Uthmān al-Naṭṭā' al-Arbalī. The Vatican Library manuscript describes instructions for constructing eleven stone talismans, while the BnF manuscript outlines thirteen.

In this article, I present a complete translation in English of this work based on the two existing Arabic manuscripts. I have combined the texts into a single, cohesive translation with the goal of achieving practical clarity while remaining as faithful as possible to the original wording and meaning.

A notion should be made regarding the talismanic letters or glyphs that are presented in both manuscripts, for they differ from each copy. To capture these differences, I have given both versions and redrawn them based on the original documents. Furthermore, to make the text as practical as possible, I have taken the liberty of creating and including in my translation digital renditions of the talismanic images that should be engraved on the stones, according to their specific description.

I hope readers will find this remarkable work engaging, as I believe it is a valuable text that deserves attention and a place in the contemporary revival of the little-known lapidary and astrological image magic literature.

The Book of Stones and Beads: Their Benefits, Testing, and Talismans by the Wise Philosopher Ptolemy

Here is the book of Ptolemy on the benefits of stones and gems, their processing, their talismanic images, the times of their making, how to work with them, how to test gems, the methods of engraving them, and their designs:

In the name of God, the Most Merciful, the Most Compassionate. Praise be to God, and may He send blessings and peace upon His Prophet Muhammad and his family. Praise be to God, and blessings upon His Messenger. With Him, we seek guidance, and to Him we ascribe unity, for He is the Helper.

Ptolemy the Wise said: "I have studied every book, each containing a category of wisdom and knowledge, and I have included in these books what is well-known, and sufficient in itself, requiring no further description. What remains for me now is the knowledge of gems and stones—their benefits, natures, different types, the times of their effectiveness, the method of preparing them and the description of how to work with them. And I will describe and explain this according to the insights and knowledge available on the subject, clarifying it, God willing."

Zumurrud—Emerald

It has two types—green and yellow.

Regarding the green one, it is taken on Wednesday when the Moon is in Aquarius and in opposition to Mars. The image of Jupiter is to be engraved on it,[2] which is a young man wearing a mantle and a loincloth or apron, raising his right hand over his head, and holding in it a fish, and he is standing on a figure of a lizard.

---

2 It should be noted that this talismanic figure of a man with his arm or hands raised, holding a fish while standing on a lizard appears in other Arabic texts on astrological magic and the properties of stones, such as *Ghāyat al-Ḥakīm* (known as *Picatrix* in Latin) by Pseudo-Maslama al-*Majrīti* and *Kitāb Khawāṣṣ al-Ahjār* by Ḥunayn ibn Isḥāq. In these texts, the figure is associated with Saturn and is to be engraved on another stone under different conditions. The reason for its association with Jupiter in Pseudo-Ptolemy's work remains unclear.

Below it, these talismanic letters should be inscribed.

MS BAV, Sbath 48	MS BnF, ar. 2772
ح و د ع	اوك

If a man wears it on his body or sets it in a ring, he will earn the favor of his ruler, and no one will precede him in his presence. His words will be heard and considered, and he will gain high dignity and great honor.

As for the yellow emerald, it is to be engraved on Saturday, while the Moon is in Capricorn, and in sextile with Jupiter at midday,[3] with an image of a man holding a spear in his hand, riding on an eagle.

Below it, these talismanic letters should be inscribed.

MS BAV, Sbath 48	MS BnF, ar. 2772
اح ط ع ه س ح	ارموع

---

3 The term *niṣfu n-nahār* means midday or midnoon, the time when the Sun is at its zenith and strongest. For reference, see *The Great Introduction to Astrology* by Abū Maʿšar (2 vols.), ed. Keiji Yamamoto and Charles Burnett. With an addition of the Greek Version by David Pingree. In an astrological context, this means the time when the Sun is in conjunction with the Midheaven (MC or Medium Coeli).

If the stone is worn as was previously described,[4] its owner will not be afraid of any harm and will not be troubled by sorrow. If anyone sought to harm the bearer, they would be unable to do so, nor could they devise any ill intent against him as long as the stone remained in his possession.

Yāqūt—Corundum

All its varieties are suitable for work and handling. It is to be engraved on Sunday when the Moon is in Sagittarius in opposition to Saturn, with the image of Venus which is in the form of a woman riding a horse, holding a shield and a halberd spear.

Below it, these talismanic letters should be inscribed.

MS BAV, Sbath 48	MS BnF, ar. 2772
ح طه حه حش ح	حمول

If everything is done as instructed and if a man wears it, he will be provided with abundant attention from women and will be favored by them. They will seek him out, their resistance toward him will diminish, and their affection for him will increase.

4 Worn or set in a ring.

Zabarjad—Peridot or Beryl[5]

Its power is immense, and its benefit is great. It is to be engraved on Tuesday when the Moon is in Libra in opposition to Mercury, with the image of Mars, which is a man with a sword in his hand as if he is striking someone.

Below it, these talismanic letters should be inscribed.

MS BAV, Sbath 48	MS BnF, ar. 2772
ح ح عمطع لاىع	ومرلاحاف

Then if a man wears it and encounters someone determined to kill him, that person's hand will be restrained as if chained unable to harm him.

'Aqīq—Agate

Both the red and yellow varieties are beneficial. It is to be engraved on Thursday, when the Moon is with Saturn in opposition to Jupiter at midday, with the image of Mercury sitting on a chair as if he is addressing a bird in the form of an eagle.

Below it, these talismanic letters should be inscribed.

---

5 Contemporary mineralogy literature defines "*zabarjad*" as peridot, a gem mined from the uninhabited Egyptian Red Sea island of Zabarjad (also known as St. John's Island), from which the stone takes its name. However, some Arabic and Persian dictionaries also define "*zabarjad*" as topaz or aquamarine. In his seminal work, *Essai sur la minéralogie arabe*, the French orientalist Jean-Jacques Clément Mullet identifies "*zabarjad*" as beryl, based on his research into al-Tīfāshī's works on stones, preserved in the French National Library.

MS BAV, Sbath 48	MS BnF, ar. 2772
[illegible]	امروں

If a man wears it on his person—whether on his finger or at his waist—anyone to whom he writes a letter (petition) will accept and fulfil his requests, even in matters as serious as blood. His words will be accepted, and he will succeed in attaining what he desires and chooses.

Khamāhan—Hematite

It is to be engraved when the Moon is in Pisces in sextile with the North Node, with an image of a man holding a bow and shooting at a crane.

Below it, these talismanic letters should be inscribed.

MS BAV, Sbath 48	MS BnF, ar. 2772
Not presented	ارككل

If a man prone to conflict, who is constantly fighting and causing turmoil and mischief, wears it on his person these tendencies will leave him, bringing calmness and a change in his nature.

Mahā—Clear Quartz[6]

The stone is to be taken and engraved on Friday right after the midday prayer (Salat Al-Jumu'a), when the Moon is in the middle of Virgo and in sextile with Jupiter, with the image of a naked man wearing a loincloth or apron as if he had leapt backwards, holding a spear in his right hand and a shield in his left hand.

Below it, these talismanic letters should be inscribed.

MS BAV, Sbath 48	MS BnF, ar. 2772

If this is done as explained, and it is worn by a man, or attached to unsellable merchandise; an animal, or something similar, it won't take long before it begins to prosper. He will soon witness the results

6 The term *al-mahā* is applied to the pure and clear white variety of the rock crystal. The Iranian polymath Al-Bīrūnī refers to the stone as quartz *(ballūr),* using the terms *al-maha'* or *al-mahu'*: "it is a word made up of *ma'* (water) and *hawa'* (air), the source of life, because [these two elements] resemble each other in their lack of colour," in *Rivers of Paradise: Water in Islamic Art and Culture* (Blair and Bloom 134). In *Moses Maimonides' Glossary of Drug Names* (Rosner 174), under the name *maha,* the following explanation is provided: "*Mahā* or *mahi* is a Persian term (potentially borrowed from Sanskrit), which, according to Vullers, designates a white crystalline stone which was hung around the neck of pregnant women to facilitate their childbirth by a magical force. Dozy explains the name *hagar al-maha* as 'crystal' or 'sapphire,' and *hagar samsi* ('sunrock') as 'girasol'. This last precious stone is a corundum which casts a great fire, particularly toward the sun. One must consider sapphire or star-stone quartz." Al-Beruni, in his Lapidary, writes *mahā, mihā, mahāh,* and *mahw* and explains these names as a type of rock-crystal. (P. Kahle and Bergkristall 325–327).

he desires and notice clear signs of success and prosperity from the moment the stone is attached.

Bahmard stone[7]

It is a greyish stone, the color of earth, found with some Kurds and called in Arabic "the stone of the righteous man Bahmard (or Baharmard)." It is to be engraved on Thursday at midday when the Moon is in Libra in opposition to Venus,[8] with an image of a naked man wearing a loincloth or apron made of tree leaves, and on his head is something resembling a long cap or hood, also made of leaves. He is leaning on a cane or a walking stick at his waist. His left hand is resting on the top of the cane, and his right hand is extended outward as if he is pointing or gesturing with it.

Below it, these talismanic letters should be inscribed.

MS BAV, Sbath 48	MS BnF, ar. 2772
خمرکـــ٧عع	احـوطکروهج

If the stone is made as explained and a person carries it with him after losing something, he will be able to find it and will not be unaware of who took it. Nothing stolen from him will remain hidden, nor will the thief. The owner of this stone should not withhold it from anyone who asks for it in order to recover what they have lost, for this will bring better results and make its use more effective.

---

7 I haven't been able to identify this stone or to find any information that clarifies what it might be. According to *The Complete Book of Muslim and Parsi Names* by Maneka Gandhi and Ozair Hussain, Bahmard is used as a given name that means a good man.

8 In MS BAV, Sbath 48 the text says: when the Moon is in Libra in sextile with Jupiter.

Lāzaward—Lapis Lazuli

One should take from this kind that has a pure color, a lot of golden specks, and a strong luster, as it is more successful. It should be engraved on Wednesday, when the Moon is in Pisces, at midday when the Sun is at its zenith,[9] with the image of a man with two wings, holding a distinguished sword in his right hand as if he has raised it to strike, and his other hand extended as if he is speaking or gesturing with it,[10] and around his waist, a loincloth or apron.

Below it, these talismanic letters should be inscribed.

MS BAV, Sbath 48	MS BnF, ar. 2772
[illegible]	[illegible]

If this is done as explained, a person can place the stone under his head and ask whatever he wishes while falling asleep. Then, in his dream, he will see the person he desires to see, whether near or far, and the person will speak to him about what is on their mind—whether it is good, evil, or otherwise. They will also express what is in their heart, whether love or hatred, and nothing about them will be hidden. If the same image is engraved on a red Bahmard stone on Monday during the hour of Jupiter, and a woman wears it, she will have influence over her husband and others, calming any anger. No one who writes it will have a need go unfulfilled.

---

9 In MS BnF, ar. 2772 the texts says: when the Moon is in Pisces in square with the Sun at midday.

10 In MS BnF, ar. 2772 the text says: in his left hand he is holding a rooster.

Jaz'—Onyx

It is to be engraved on Thursday, when the Moon is in Gemini in sextile with Mars at midday, with the image of Venus standing on a cow and holding in it a halberd, with a depiction of a lion on it.

Below it, these talismanic letters should be inscribed.

MS BAV, Sbath 48	MS BnF, ar. 2772
[illegible]	كاوع

If it is worn by a woman who has had difficulty getting married, and men have sought her hand, she will get married, her obstacles will be removed, and her desirability will increase.

It should not be worn by her while she is menstruating or when there is anything impure on her, but rather after purification. She should pour over herself water that has been boiled with pomegranate, myrtle,[11] and safflower while it is still warm. She should wear a clean garment and then hang the stone on her left upper arm in the prescribed manner.

Billawr—Quartz/Rock Crystal[12]

A precious stone that corresponds to the essence of its existence and its natural nobility. It is to be engraved while Pisces is rising and when the Moon is in Libra in opposition to Mercury at midday,

---

11 The plant is likely myrtle, as it is associated with Venus, and in Arabic, the word *"raiḥân"* refers to both basil and myrtle as aromatic plants.

12 In the Persian and Arab mineralogical treatises, rock crystal (quartz) is denoted with the name *ballūr* or *billawr*, which comes from the Greek word *bérulos/beryllion* for beryl, but underwent reallocation in Arabic to specifically indicate rock crystal.

the image of Venus depicted as a naked woman who appears to be pulling something out of her left foot with tweezers, with a coiled snake on her head and another on her leg.

Below it, these talismanic letters should be inscribed.

MS BAV, Sbath 48	MS BnF, ar. 2772
[illegible]	[illegible]

If this is done as explained, and the man wears it on his body, it will reduce his desire for intercourse, and he will not be concerned with it or commit any sin. It will protect him from seeking corruption, and even if he remains for a thousand years with a thousand maidens, his heart will not incline towards them as long as it is hanging on him. It should be worn around the man's waist.

Magnāṭis—Magnetite

It is of two types: black, which attracts iron, and speckled, which does not attract iron.

The speckled one, which has a lot of white, should be taken on Wednesday when the Moon is in Taurus. It is to be engraved with the image of the zodiac circle of the twelve signs, with Mars in the center, holding a sword in his hand, and under his feet is a serpent. In his other hand, he is holding a pommel, and on his little finger, a whip or a knocker.[13]

13 The exact meaning here is somewhat ambiguous, as "pommel" could refer to a knob on a sword hilt or the raised part at the front of a saddle, while the term translated as "whip" could also mean "knocker." My interpretation is that the figure holds a metal knocker with a pommel, similar to a door clapper.

Below it, these talismanic letters should be inscribed.

MS BAV, Sbath 48	MS BnF, ar. 2772
[illegible]	[illegible]

If this is done as explained with the stone, a man places it under his head and asks about what he desires while falling asleep. He calls the names of the person he wants and loves, the one who occupies his heart, or someone he cannot hope to be with while awake. Then, he sleeps on his left side, and during his sleep, a vision of that person will come to him, staying with him in every amusement and pleasure, that soothes his heart's longing. The person will stay with him until the end of the night and quell the fire of his desire. Then, the vision will bid him farewell and depart. When the man wakes up, he will remember what he experienced, and his heart will be at peace. He can do this every night if he wishes to see the person in his dreams.

Jamast—Amethyst

It is to be engraved on Saturday, when the Moon is in Pisces forming a square to the North Node, with the image of a beardless boy holding a spear and a shield in his left hand, with his hands gathered towards the shield, and his hand raised above his head,[14] while his face is turned backward. He is holding a gazelle leg in his right hand.

14 In this part, the writing in the manuscript is unclear due to staining, making it difficult to determine whether the figure holds the shield with one hand or both, which hand is raised, and what exactly are the objects it carries. The overall meaning is ambiguous, so I offer my interpretation of how I understand it.

Below it, these talismanic letters should be inscribed.

MS BAV, Sbath 48	MS BnF, ar. 2772
Not presented	[illegible]

This is a charm for affection. It does not take long for this talisman to take effect on the desired person, until he comes to the owner of the stone. And he will be under his complete control, at his hands and feet. It is necessary to write beneath the stone the name of the desired person and the name of his mother.

Specifying the Testing of Stones and Which Ones Are Suitable for Work and Processing

- **Emerald**: One of the tests for pure, high-quality emerald is, if a snake catches sight of it, tears flow from its eyes.
- **Corundum:** Its test lies in its permanence; you will find it cool at all times, both in summer and winter.
- **Peridot or Beryl:** Its test is when a gray or blue mouse sees it, it continuously dances and strikes its face with its paws as long as it remains in front of it.
- **Agate:** If rubbed with water and salt, its polished surface emerges rosy and clear.
- **Hematite:** When rubbed with water and salt, it comes out white like milk, and that is what is suitable for work.
- **Onyx**: If rubbed with water, its polished surface turns a dark hue, which indicates its high quality.
- **Quartz/Rock crystal:** When rubbed with water, it turns red like porphyry; this is the high-quality type suitable for work, and none other.

- **Clear quartz:** When rubbed with Andarani water and salt,[15] it turns slightly blue, which indicates its high quality. If it turns white or red, it is unsuitable.
- **Bahmard stone:** The stone appearing grayish, the color of earth. When rubbed with water and porphyry, its polished surface turns white, like the color of milk, with a soft texture, making it suitable for processing.
- **Lapis lazuli:** If rubbed with water and whiteness,[16] its color turns black, and if the polish is soft, then it is suitable for processing.
- **Magnetite:** The speckled variety is rubbed with the saliva (secretion) of psyllium seeds, resulting in a clear green polish with hard texture. When it reaches this state, it is considered high-quality and ideal for effective work.

---

15 A variety of rock salt imported from a village in al-Sham (Syria) known as Andara.

16 The exact meaning of the word is unclear, as it could refer to the color white, a whitening agent, or a substance like albumen or an alkaline compound.

Bibliography

Amar, Zohar and Lev Efraim. "Most-Cherished Gemstones in the Medieval Arab World." *Journal of the Royal Asiatic Society*, vol. 27, no. 3, 2017.

"Arabe 2772." *Archives et Manuscrits*, National Library of France (BnF), https://archivesetmanuscrits.bnf.fr/ark:/12148/cc30685b.

Blair, Sheila and Jonathan Bloom. *Rivers of Paradise: Water in Islamic Art and Culture.* Yale University Press, 2009.

Clément-Mullet, J. J. "Essai sur la Minéralogie Arabe." *Journal Asiatique*, vol. 6, 1868.

Contadini, Anna. "Facets of Light: The Case of Rock Crystals." *God is the Light of the Heavens and the Earth. Light in Islamic Art and Culture*, Yale University Press, 2015.

Gandhi, Maneka, and Ozair Husain. *The Complete Book of Muslim and Parsi Names.* Penguin Books India, 2004.

Kahle, Paul. "Bergkristall, Glas und Glasflüsse nach dem Steinbuch von el-Beruni." *Morgen L. Geselschaft*, vol. 90, 1936, pp. 325–327.

Lecouteux, Claude. *A Lapidary of Sacred Stones: Their Magical and Medicinal Powers Based on the Earliest Sources.* Inner Traditions, 2012.

Maimonides, Moses. *Glossary of Drug Names.* The Maimonides Research Institute, 1995.

Rovati, Emanuele. "Pseudo-Ptolemy, Kitāb al-Aḥjār." *Ptolemaeus Arabus et Latinus*, 2025, http://ptolemaeus.badw.de/work/266.

"Sbath 48." *DigiVatLib*, Biblioteca Apostolica Vaticana, https://digi.vatlib.it/view/MSS_Sbath.48.

Yamamoto, Keiji, and Charles Burnett, translator. *The Great Introduction to Astrology by Abū Maʿšar (2 Vols.).* Brill, 2019.

At the Crossroads

Exploring Central Balkan Magic in Modern Practice

by Katerina Sarpione

In a secluded village, tucked away somewhere in the Central Balkans, a small and rather ordinary house is surrounded by numerous cars, with plate registrations from all over the country. It is the house of an old healer, bound by blood and oath to help those in need, whenever they come. The healer still practises the ancient craft of molybdomancy. The old healer may melt wax instead of lead, or perhaps she's skilled in favomancy—divining by means of dried beans. It is highly possible that she only uses her secret spoken charms and nothing else. Nevertheless, even in this age of technology, people still seek the healer and, equally, her darker counterpart—the witch, who brings her own ancient knowledge to those who call. In the heart of the Balkans, magic is not confined to legends—it is alive, whispering through ancient rites and echoing in the minds of those who still abide by the traditions. It is thus a bit paradoxical that when we look to younger magical practitioners, this living tradition is not reflected in their practice at all. In its place we find some rendition of either the Western or Eastern traditions. Sometimes, both at the same time.

The Balkans have been a crossroads of cultures since ancient times, well before the notion of the West and East took shape.

Situated roughly where the continents of Europe, Asia, and Africa meet, with access to the seas, mountains, and fields, and having a moderate climate, appropriate for both agriculture and animal husbandry, it was a natural choice for numerous people throughout history to settle in. And the land and customs still bear signs of their presence. From the unknown prehistoric rites, through the mysteries of the Thracians, Macedonians, and ancient Greeks, to the various teachings of Christianity and Islam, the culture of the Central Balkans bears the traces of many beliefs. The centuries of Orthodox Christianity dominance have made the strongest mark and shaped firm beliefs about heaven, hell, and the soul's journey. Nevertheless, many ancient, pre-Christian notions about the afterlife still persist in folk traditions.

The Central Balkans encompass the heart of southeastern Europe, where the cultural crossroads have shaped folklore and magical practices for centuries. Generally, this region includes modern-day Serbia, North Macedonia, Bulgaria, Montenegro, and Kosovo—countries with shared beliefs yet distinct local nuances. In the following pages, you will have the opportunity to explore a small part of these magical practices, most of them coming from the heart of the Central Balkans—the territory of nowadays Bulgaria. That being said, it's crucial to recognize that holding onto the past alone is neither practical nor realistic. Times change, so do magical practices. While keeping the tradition alive is important, it should not be done blindly. I no longer have the need to protect my crops from witches, because (sadly) I do not own any fields. But in the spells of the past lies a certain wisdom that can still be valuable in our modern life. Magic is current when it is useful. Thus, you'll find some practical approaches to translating the magic of the Balkans into your own modern practice. But first, we need to establish a few foundational concepts that have shaped Balkan magic for generations.

Folklore and Worldview

There has to be a disclaimer in every book about folklore, or mythology for that matter, that warns that it is never a stable, invariable, and unified system. What scholars capture is merely a still frame in an ongoing story. That being said, there are certain patterns that can be observed and, subsequently, modified to everyone's own individual life. In essence, with some small exceptions, that was what people before us did anyway—that is where the folk in folklore comes from.

Though ethnographic studies detail many specific rites and traditions of the Central Balkans, our journey begins with the songs. Not so long ago, people used to sing all the time—there was a song for every daily activity, for every celebration, and for expressing their beliefs about the world. The numerous songs were one of the first traces of folk culture that people began to gather during the nineteenth century, when contemporary ethnography had its genesis. Thus, most of the magical beliefs of old reach us in the form of songs. Despite the diversity in folk beliefs, there is a common idea that the world is not a single entity but is divided into separate parts or even distinct worlds. This concept is well-reflected in folk songs, where the division of the world between the saints is a recurring theme, though with varying outcomes:

First, they decided for Saint Elijah,
Set aside for him the earth in its depths,
And they set aside for him the sky in its heights,
And they set aside for him the fearful thunders.
After him, they decided for Saint Nicholas,
And granted him his rightful portion—
They set aside for him the waters and the crossings.
After him, they decided for Saint Archangel Michael,
Set aside for him the souls of the people (Staliyski 24).

This part of a song, from the Serbian village Vlasi near Pirot, is only one rendition of this popular theme. The saints and the realms they divide between each other slightly vary in different versions, but broadly speaking, the world can be divided into several principal parts:

- The earth, where humans and other earthly creatures live.
- The water, which is the source of life, but also home to wondrous beings.
- The sky, where the celestial lights shine and the dwellings of God are located.
- The Beyond, where the souls of the dead wander.

However, these separate realms often merge, and the beings that inhabit them frequently wander between them. On the other hand, as we have already established, there are no clear or universally applicable criteria by which to arrange these realms in neat order. The realms intertwine, just as our fates intertwine with one another, and this is the most natural thing. For there to be order, there must also be chaos. And vice versa. While the different realms in the folklore of the Central Balkans might be elusive, there is a lot to be said about the entities that are believed to inhabit it.

On a more mundane level, we will find that there is a stark difference between the world we inhabit and the Beyond, where the souls of the dead wander. In Balkan culture, the realms of the living and the dead are meant to stay separate, but it is believed that the deceased continue to influence our lives, whether as protectors, messengers, or—if certain rituals are neglected—dangerous entities capable of bringing misfortune. This has led to elaborate funerary practices and regular rites for appeasing the dead, which, in some form, are still practiced today.

Similar to the Beyond is the realm believed to lie at the edge of the world, where mythical creatures and wild animals retreat in tune with the changing seasons. One of the most captivating beings inhabiting this realm is the anthropomorphic female *samo-*

diva (Bulgarian, pl. *samodivi*). Known by other names across the Balkans—such as *samovila* (Bulgarian/Macedonian), *vila* (Bulgarian/Serbian/Montenegrin), *yuda* (Bulgarian), or *zana* (Albanian)—she is a figure of great beauty and power. In some traditions, she merges with other mythical entities, reflecting the fluid nature of Balkan folklore (Yorova 37). A *samodiva* is a powerful entity, bound to the wilderness and similar to the nymphs, that acts both in benevolent and malevolent ways. Most often, the *samodiva* appears as a young, extremely beautiful woman with long, generally blonde hair that floats while she walks or moves. She is dressed in a white garment, thin as a shadow, making her youthful body almost visible. On her waist she has a belt with the colours of the rainbow, with green being the predominant one. A *samodiva* is almost never alone, but does everything in a group with her sisters and friends—they sing and dance together, they bathe together, they fly together (Marinov 294).

Another mythical creature worth mentioning is the dragon-like *zmey* (Bulgarian), *zmaj* (Serbian/Montenegrin), or *dragoj* (Albanian), who inhabits secluded caves and high mountain peaks. The *zmey* has a dualistic nature—he is mostly considered a benevolent being, oftentimes serving as a protector of villages. At the same time, he is believed to have the ability to turn into a beautiful young man and seduce young women, who would slowly begin to fade and ultimately—if left untreated—would die, joining him in his otherworldly realm (Marinov 302–303). A similar serpentine creature is the female *hala* (Bulgarian), *ala* (Serbian/Macedonian), or *kuçedra* (Albanian), which, contrary to the *zmey*, is perceived only as a malevolent figure. Some describe her as a massive lizard with a dog's head capable of swallowing an ox, or as a "three-headed, six-winged, twelve-tailed serpent," or even as a huge snake with seven or nine heads. Her main goal is to harm people, most of the time stealing all the water or damaging their crops with hail (Marinov 306–307).

The heart of the Balkans has always been a cultural crossroad, which has resulted in the worship of diverse deities. Most modern practitioners are familiar with the ancient Hellenic deities, whose influence extended into this region, often blending with the gods and goddesses of the Illyrians, Thracians, and, in later periods, Romans. Over time, the arrival of new tribes and peoples introduced their own pantheons and beliefs, enriching the spiritual tapestry of the region. The almost perpetual arrival of new tribes, among which were Celts, Slavs, Avars, Bulgars, and later Ottomans, contributed to further enrichment of the local spiritual traditions. Over time, many of these pagan deities merged with Christian saints and Islamic holy figures, creating a unique blend of religious beliefs. This complex heritage offers modern practitioners a wealth of deities, deeply rooted in the land's history, to connect with in their spiritual work.

While this blend of beliefs offers a rich spiritual foundation, it's important to remember that much of the folklore we rely on today comes from data gathered by ethnographers some 70 to almost 200 years ago. It is obvious that time has passed, and many habits, customs, and everyday activities have changed. I want to emphasise that this change was much, much more rapid than any other change in previous historical periods. With immense advancements in science and technology, it's natural to question the relevance of these spirits today. Why should one fear a spirit that harms crops with hail, or wonder if woodland spirits exist amidst city traffic? Ultimately, what role, if any, do these spirits play in modern life?

Traditional Magic

Understanding the historical basis of these practices gives us a foundation to adapt them to today's world, ensuring they remain meaningful and relevant. In order to do that, we need to look back at what significance spirits and traditions held before fading into dusty books and scholarly studies. It is always challenging to capture the role of folklore in everyday life and magical practice, given the difference between how folklore was once lived versus how it's accessed now. While today we actively seek out folklore—flipping through books and studying archived stories—people in the past were immersed in it daily, with no clear division between everyday life, magic, religion, and superstition. The existence of non-human entities was rarely questioned; they were simply accepted as real as stones or rivers, even if they remained unseen. This perception may have stemmed from a life more intimately connected to nature, where people relied not only on their physical senses but also on their intuition and gut instincts.

Back then, life's rhythm was closely tied to the land and seasons, and people's roles were grounded in family and community, nurturing a connection to the natural and unseen worlds that is often missing today. Witches and healers existed within this integrated worldview as intermediaries, guides, and keepers of knowledge. One of the first Bulgarian ethnographers, the priest, Petar Lyubenov, would reluctantly write in 1887:

> *The witches and charm healers among the common folk are held in such high regard that neither the priest nor the teacher enjoys the same level of respect. If someone falls ill, the family will immediately rush to the witch to have him extinguish water in a bowl or to chant a spell over them. If someone loses something, they will run to the charm healer to have her tell them where it is and who has taken it. If someone is unable to marry, they go to the charm healer to find out what is causing the misfortune and how to proceed to achieve success. In short, for any situation, people turn to the witch and charm healer for guidance and advice, as if they are people who know everything. Therefore, upon approaching them, out of respect, people kneel and kiss their hand and knee...(56–57).*

But this respect wasn't without an edge of fear. Known for healing, divining, and offering guidance, these folk magic practitioners could also use their abilities to protect, punish, or destroy. Among scholars, there is a consensus that the folk healer and the witch were perceived in different ways. The healer was revered for their benevolence—often serving as not only the sole medical help for both people and animals, but also as a wise elder in the community. Contrarily, the witch was regarded with disdain for their malevolence and, in some cases, it was believed that they did evil just for the sake of it (Mishev 72, 93). While this does reflect an existing attitude in the Central Balkans, there is something to be said about the amount of information that reaches scholars.

Ethnographic records of magical practices, customs, and rituals in the region began to be gathered systematically during the nineteenth century. Some of the folk healers, who were open about their practice, were eager to share it, but we could only guess at what parts they intentionally excluded. The witches, on the other hand, were people who would most often practise in secret and would very rarely share their spells, because of how that could affect their social standing. Truth be told, we will never know if the healer and witch were as separate as scholars have accepted. What we do know is that in times of trouble, either the witch or the folk healer were called upon to wield power in ways that matched the community's needs, whether benign or vengeful. Understanding their role in society means understanding that they were known for being able to pivot from aid to punishment, from protection to retribution. That being said, there is still a stark difference in the attitude towards a person determined to help and one that is adamant to do harm.

The folk healer was sought mostly for helping cure children and aid in dealing with illnesses that were either hard or impossible to treat. In a time when people suffered a very high percentage of child mortality and even a flu could end in death, the role of the healer was not only to heal, but to bring hope, too. Most of the healing is performed through chants or incantations, generally called *baene* in Bulgarian and *bajanje* in Serbian, Macedonian, Montenegrin, and Kosovo Albanian. A large number of the preserved chants are for healing fear or the evil eye, known as *uroki* in Bulgarian and *uroci* in the other Central Balkan languages. The evil eye in the whole Balkan peninsula is widely perceived as a real, serious threat and to this day, many people take precautions and seek treatment when they are not successful in avoiding it. The general cause of the evil eye is when someone looks at you with ill intent. There are a lot of reasons for catching *uroki* and not all of them are intentional. For instance, it is a common belief that people with blue eyes or those that were re-nursed after weaning cause *uroki*, even if they are genuinely friendly (Todorova-Pirgova 109). Another major cause of illness is when a person gets scared of something. Distress like that is believed to shift the very essence of a person and cause him even physical unease. Thankfully, there are a lot of ways to remedy such conditions, and a good example is this healing incantation from the region of Parvomay, Bulgaria.

Incantation for Healing the Evil Eye

When someone, whether a child or an elder, is believed to be afflicted by the evil eye, they visit the folk healer for help. She leads them outside to the yard, and while rubbing their forehead with the thumb of her right hand, silently chants:

> *In the name of the Holy Mother of God, may the evil go to the place where roosters do not crow, where dogs do not bark, where birds do not live, where trees do not grow, where water does not flow, where neither the sun nor the moon shine—to desolate forests, desolate places, and barren stones!*

She repeats the chant three times. Then, she washes the person's face with cold water, into which the chant has been spoken three times, and gives them a sip of that water before sending them home (Popov 78–79).

A similar incantation from Pirdop, North Macedonia gives a more vivid description.

For Healing Fear by Means of Melting Lead

The healer prepares a small clay bowl filled with water drawn from a well. Into the water, she places nine grains of barley, dropping them one by one and counting backward: "Nine, eight, seven, six, five, four, three, two, one, without one." Afterward, she adds three crumbs of bread to the bowl, counting in the same manner. She then melts small pieces of lead in a metal container designated solely for this purpose. While the lead melts over the fire, she recites the following words:

> *Her/his fear, her/his harm. The forest was startled, the water was startled, the sky was startled, the earth was startled. The forest remained, the water remained, the sky remained, the earth remained.*

She repeats this incantation three times. Once the lead is fully melted, she pours it into the bowl of water above the head of the frightened person to observe the shapes it forms. The figure in the lead is said to reveal the source of the fear. She repeats this process three times—once above the head, once near the heart, and once at the knees. At the end of the ritual, the healer gives the person three sips of the water from the bowl and washes their eyes with it. The melted lead is given to the person to sleep with for three nights, after which it must be thrown into a river early in the morning on the third day (Todorova-Pirgova 197–198).

Healing rituals are aimed at helping others, and oftentimes the healer is bound by oath to accept anyone at any time. It is a common belief that the ability to heal is something one should not keep for themselves, otherwise they could suffer punishment from God. It is appropriate to mention that most of the healers consider themselves to be pious Christians or Muslims and would be offended if someone even hints otherwise. These Abrahamic religions have blended so well into the folk practices that they are oftentimes inseparable.

Oddly enough, the same can be said about the maleficent practices, known as black magic. But while in western Europe the Devil has been considered the main source of power for witches, in the Central Balkans the witch mostly relies on patron saints, harnesses her own power, or, alternatively, steals the potency of others. In the past, stealing the fertility of other people's fields and livestock constituted a large part of the repertoire of a Balkan witch, but stealing the power of the Moon was the epitome of being such a witch. The idea that witches harvest the power of the Moon is not a new one and has been around literally for millenia (Edmonds III 19–21). Unfortunately, there is no preserved detailed description of the way the witches in the Central Balkans performed that magic. But even the fragments that we have can tell us an evocative story—how a witch draws down the Moon and, in the guise of a cow, milks it (Mishev 109). But apart from these rather enchanting accounts of the witch, she does some everyday work as well.

Love Spell

If you wish for someone to like you, you must find milk from a mother and daughter who are both nursing. The milk is mixed with flour to knead a dough, which is then baked into a round loaf with a hole in the centre. Once the loaf is ready, you must look through its hole with your right eye, focusing on the person of your desire. While doing this, you say the following words three times:

As the mother and daughter cannot be separated,
And as their milk cannot be divided,
So may you never be able
To part from me! (Todorova-Pirgova 463)

Truth be told, binding your beloved with the power of breast-milk might not be considered particularly malevolent nowadays. However, the darker side of Balkan magic offers far more chilling rituals—those aimed at harming or even destroying one's enemies.

Curse for Illness and Death

To perform this spell, take a brick and place it under the eaves of a house where water drips. Light four candles at the brick's corners, positioning the wicks downward. While the candles burn, recite the names of your enemies—whether by nickname, family name, or the name they are known by in the village—and then say the following words:

[All the names],
all known and unknown enemies,
who have caused me harm,
may they burn and melt,
may they die and wither;
may they turn to dust,
may they turn to earth!
Saint Mina, Holy Mother of God,
and the Almighty—may they not forgive them!

Once the spell is complete, throw the brick, along with the remains of the candles, at a crossroads outside the village (Todorova-Pirgova 477–478). According to canon, St. Mina is a male saint, but in folklore, likely due to the feminine form of the name, he is often perceived as a female saint. Both healers and witches honor this folkloric version of St. Mina as their patron, believing she provides great help in undoing harm and offers protection from evil people.

Spells like these make it quite obvious as to why people who were able to wield magic commanded both respect and fear. In a society where scarcity often meant literal death, the ability to magically redistribute abundance, fertility, and health, was a very real threat and thus—a most valuable skill. While these blessings are still valid today, the world we live in is very different. Some historical and folkloric practices may seem odd, irrelevant, or even offensive by today's standards when removed from the complex cultural context of their own time. For instance, we no longer mortally fear the bubonic plague, so the customs and rituals for the chasing away of its respective demonic entity are no longer of use to us. But there is a lot of wisdom in such practices, either magical or mundane ones, that lies beneath their immediate practicality. The tricky part is developing the cultural understanding and adaptability needed to harness it.

Such skills came naturally to those who were part of the traditional cultures, meaning they had, without the need to learn it actively, the understanding of the mechanisms behind the spell or the rite. The term "folk witchcraft" reflects this—every person who changed a spell did it without the help of the full editions of occult literature available at the time. The inability to read paradoxically served as an advantage for our ancestors, because they did not feel the pressure to live up to Heinrich Cornelius Agrippa, Aleister Crowley, Doreen Valiente, or whoever was considered knowledgeable at the time. They had to be able to understand the magic from memory, experience, and adaptability. Nowadays, most of us need to gradually develop these skills through the study of documented practices, as well as by understanding the broader historical, geographical, and social context in which these practices arose and were used. Ethnographic and anthropological research is, of course, invaluable, as scholars work to uncover how and why magical actions played such a crucial role in the societies of the past. A huge advantage is being born in the culture—an immersion that is irreplaceable. Growing up within a specific culture provides nuances that sadly books or even videos are unable to fully replicate. This does not mean you cannot engage meaningfully with the craft of a given place, even if you have never been there. Deep research and a sincere effort to understand the cultural framework can foster a meaningful and authentic connection with the craft in question. Yet, in today's fast-paced world, it can be challenging for modern magical practitioners to dedicate the time needed even to spark their curiosity on the subject. In the case of Balkan magic, as with many other folk practices, the resources available in English are limited, posing an even greater challenge for those unfamiliar with the local languages. But by exploring these sources and methods of adaptation, we can bring the wisdom of Balkan magic into contemporary practice.

Practical Applications

What follows are some simple aspects of Balkan traditional magical practices that you can implement in your own practice—either as a foundation or as an experiment. While there are strictly guarded practices in the Balkans, most of what I've included here is based on the everyday life of ordinary people. The basis of the following practices lies in history, however it needs to be said that they are modern adaptations.

In historical or reconstructionist practices, you'll inevitably encounter the idea that, for people of the past, religion and magic were inseparable from daily life. Today, we have become so accustomed to organising and labelling every aspect of our lives that this integrated approach can feel foreign. For rural elders I have met, magic was not something extraordinary, but simply part of how they navigate the world. They even found it strange when I obsessed over practices that, for them, were just trivial.

This modern tendency to label and catalogue everything, while being totally understandable and in line with our current lives, often leads to an unnecessary division between magic and life. Hanging a picture of a predecessor becomes "ancestral worship," a prayer becomes "deity devotion," and we hesitate in trying a spell from another culture, fearing accusations of cultural appropriation. While respect for ancestors, deities, and other cultures is crucial, this mindset risks turning magic into something rigid and disconnected from daily living. It's equally important to recognize that traditions evolve through exchange and adaptation, as seen in the practices of the Central Balkans. The very idea of a cultural crossroads reminds us that magic, life, and culture are fluid, resisting absolute categories of local versus foreign, good versus bad, or magic versus mundane. Truth is that we are more alike than we like to admit—walking on the same Earth, looking at the same stars.

In the Central Balkans, this shared connection manifests most vividly through the reverence for natural forces like the Sun and the Moon. While the Moon tends to receive more attention in modern witchcraft, perhaps due to its millennia-old association with nocturnal rituals, the Sun was praised by everyone in the past. The great power of the Sun as the reason for our collective existence was recognised early in human history, placing it in the centre of most of the annual celebrations around the globe. This remained true for millenia in the Balkans, and even in the beginning of the twentieth century, in some places people still believed that the Sun "is our God and saint, it gives life, protects us from evil, and when it sets we become orphans without a guardian" (Georgieva 31). It was a common thing to start work in the fields before sunrise, so greeting the sun at its first appearance for the day came naturally. People would stop their work, face the Sun, make the sign of the cross, and utter "Dear Sun!" or "Come God and help us!" Simple gestures like these not only acknowledge the important role of the fiery celestial sphere, but also seek its blessing and protection. Such customs can inspire modern practitioners, reminding us that even simple acts of reverence can hold profound meaning.

Greeting the Sun

At the first instance you see the Sun, face it (closing your eyes if needed) and say: "Dear Sun, may you bring light and warmth to my day!" Make the sign of the cross if it feels right—after all, the equal cross was a solar symbol centuries before Christianity.

Greeting the Moon

In the evening, when the Moon is visible, look at it and say: "Dear Lady of the Night, may your blessing be upon me!"

In the Balkans, the Sun is generally considered male and the Moon female, reflecting both linguistic gender and their association with traditional masculine and feminine qualities. That being said, this is not always the case—for instance, the Moon is male in Serbian and, in some cases, in Bulgarian. Feel free to adapt these words to reflect your personal relationship with them; the key is showing respect.

Honouring Your Ancestors

Just as the Sun and Moon connect us to the universe, our ancestors connect us to the land and its history. The most widespread form of ancestor veneration in the Balkans are the rituals performed during the days dedicated to commemorating the dead. In Bulgaria and Serbia, we call these days *zadushnitsa,* in Greece they are known as *psihosavato,* and there are similar commemorative days throughout the peninsula. Although the names differ, these days always fall on a Saturday before a major Orthodox Christian celebration. This generally consists of visiting the graves of your relatives and sharing food with the community in honour of the deceased. Traditionally, the grave itself serves as the ancestor altar in the Balkans. It is the place for communication with the dead and for hosting feasts in their honor.

Of course, in this global world we live in, there is a great chance that you do not have access to the graves of your predecessors. Many people with Balkan heritage no longer live in the region, and some have never even visited. Fortunately, there are still ways to connect with your ancestors even from afar. Acquire spring water either from nature or from the local grocery. Find a fruit tree, in the roots of which you could pour this water and where you could have some form of privacy. Before you do so, say something along the line of, "In the name of (say the ancestor names you know), and all the nameless ancestors who came before me, I pour this offering so that you don't walk thirsty in the Beyond." You can add a light to illuminate their nights, or some other food or beverage of choice if you feel like it and if the place allows it. Offerings depend on the spirits who are to receive them. For instance, it is quite common to light a cigarette for the dead who used to smoke and let it burn on its own (in a controlled environment, of course), while you commune with the spirits, treating them as if they are present.

The fruit tree is chosen as a symbolic link between fertility and death—its roots dig deep into the earth, while its branches bear luscious fruit under the sky. This connection has long been observed by our predecessors. It is no coincidence that in ancient Greek myth, the ruler of the Underworld and the goddess of spring growth are united as a divine pair, reflecting the belief that the Underworld itself is a source of life and fertility. After all, every seed has its beginning in the darkness of the soil.

Sharing a meal is not only reserved for communication with spirits, though. It is customary to offer food to the community in honor of the deceased. This practice reflects the belief that sharing food ensures it reaches the otherworld, allowing the spirits of the dead to enjoy it. Even today, this tradition is alive as people distribute food to their neighbors, coworkers, or relatives as part of commemorative rituals. Getting together as a community at the table is so universal that it might be considered one of the basic human traditions. It has been and still continues to be one of the central aspects of Balkan culture. So, if you want to incorporate a bit of Balkan magic—get in the habit of organising shared meals for your community no matter how small or large it might be.

Honouring Your Community

While the character of the food served would depend on the season and region, there are certain things that are rather universal. One is that no ritual meal on the Balkans is ever without three things—bread, wine, and salt. The Bulgarian ethnographer Dimitar Marinov will go so far as to say that these three things are the "ritual St. Trinity, without which no rite is performed" (213). Some observant readers might be alarmed by the lack of *rakija*—a beloved, local brandy-like spirit. Although *rakija* is indeed part of some rites, wine persists in time as the ultimate ritual beverage in the Balkans due to its complex symbolism and colour, which is reminiscent of blood and, by extension, life.

Now that you've placed bread, salt, and wine on your festive table, you need to focus on the main dish. This is the place where vegetarians might be disappointed, because the number one ritual food in the Balkans is roasted or boiled meat in numerous variations. Nevertheless, you can prepare whatever you want. Trying a traditional Balkan recipe would be nice, too.

The final step is to gather your community and share the meal, preferably on some specific date. It is customary for people here to organise such gatherings on the date which they successfully survived after an unexpected accident, disease, or misfortune. The food being a sacrifice given in gratitude for the second life they are living. There are no special words, no complex rituals here, because maintaining a healthy community is the difficult part of this rite, as many of you probably have already experienced. We live in a time when it seems like most people have ill intent towards us. Thankfully, there is a spell for that.

Protective Charms

Material magical objects depend significantly on where, when, how, and who will be using them. Thus, this section will include two common types of verbal formulae for you to experiment with.

The first formula is one that mothers use to protect their children from the evil eye before going out each day. They would touch their genitals and say, "Whoever sees my shame, let them be able to cast an evil eye on my child!". It is worth being reminded that in a traditional society, that was something extremely improbable. This is the reason why the vagina is called "shame" in this chant. But nowadays, the improbable situation included in the chant might need some adaptation. That being said, with proper phrasing, the formula can be used by anybody:

Whoever (does this), let them be able to (cast a spell) on (me)!

For instance, touch your hair and say:

Whoever counts the hairs on my head, let them be able to bind me!

The second formula also depends on the improbability of things, but it allows for the addition of some material to the gestures and words. It works in a similar way, but it evokes time.

When (this happens), then may (this befall on me)!

For instance, take a small piece of shed snake skin, a wooden charcoal, and a dried basil leaf. As you place them into a small protective bag of your choice, say:

When this snake comes to life,
When this tree bears leaves again,
When this basil puts out flowers,
Then may the spells of my enemies
Be able to reach me!

A lot of things that are considered apotropaic in Balkan folklore hold similar significance in other places—red thread, blue eye beads (*nazar*), garlic, salt, iron, silver, different plants. If you want to prepare a wearable protective charm, you might want to make a red thread with a blue bead. If you want to make one for the house, you can place additional things on that red thread, like garlic cloves in odd numbers, iron nails, or a twig of hawthorn (*Crataegus*). Research your options and experiment.

Prayer

Contemporary magical practitioners seem to be a bit afraid of prayer, probably due to the fact that most of them have been brought up Christian and still consider prayer solely an Abrahamic practice. It is not. Calling to the forces beyond our understanding is universal, regardless of how you name that. A prayer is a verbal manifestation of faith that brings us closer to what we believe in. If you would like to experiment with prayer in Balkan context, you might want to lean on the ancient formulas, attested in Hellenic sources. A good example is shared by author Mierzwicki in his book on Greek polytheism and which I've shortened for ease:

Hear me,
(list relevant epithets or titles of deity or spirit)
(insert request or state gratitude)! (73–74)

As was mentioned earlier, the Balkans have always been a cultural crossroad where diverse deities were worshipped. While you can worship any of them outside of the geographic region, in order to connect with the local Balkan spirits, you will have to be physically there. That is not a reason to make expensive travel arrangements, but a reminder that the magic of place should be respected. If you live outside of the Balkans, it would be much more fruitful to make an effort to connect with the local spirits of your own place.

Conclusion

In a busy town, far away from the Balkans and maybe even outside of Europe, in a rather large building, situated among other similarly large buildings, one person in comfortable clothes is reading about Balkan magic. They have been on a journey of reconnecting to their Balkan ancestors, or maybe they just want to explore new folk traditions from around the world. That modern person might just be curious, as we all should be, about the world around them. It is highly possible that they have had some experience with other traditions, systems, and practices. Nevertheless, even in this age of technology, that person still longs for a spiritual link with the world they inhabit.

But, after all, what role, if any, do all these spirits, deities, and traditional folk beliefs have in modern life? For those drawn to traditional folk magic, the allure may lie in its earthy, grounded nature—its reverence for the land, its recognition of the cycles of life and death, and its pragmatic approach to the unseen world. But its real power is in its ability to connect us to something greater than ourselves. Whether it's through honoring ancestors, acknowledging the spirits of the land, or simply pausing to marvel at the Sun and Moon, traditional practices encourage us to find our place in connection to the world.

The Central Balkans, a region shaped by centuries of migration, conquest, and cultural exchange, have always been a crossroad. People of countless tribes, nations, and faiths have passed through this land, leaving behind traces of their stories, beliefs, and magic while taking pieces of it with them. Being inspired by the past, while actively living in the present, is a constant reminder that magic, like culture itself, is not static but alive, evolving with each new generation that engages with it. The spirits and traditions of the Central Balkans are not yet relics of the past. Engaging in magical practices inspired by the past grants us means to connect—with our ancestors, with the land, and ultimately—with ourselves. We just have to realize that past, present, and future, like the different paths of a road, often blend and overlap, forming the crossroads where the magical practitioner must stand.

Bibliography

Edmonds III, Radcliffe G. *Drawing Down the Moon: Magic in the Ancient Greco-Roman World.* Princeton University Press, 2019.

Георгиева, Иваничка. *Българска народна митология.* АИ "Проф. Марин Дринов", София, 2018. [Georgieva, Ivanichka. *Balgarska narodna mitologia.* AI "Prof. Marin Drinov", Sofia, 2018.]

Любенов, Петър. *Баба Ега или сборник от различни вярвания, народни лекувания, магии, баяния и обичаи в Кюстендилско.* Търново, 1887. [Lyubenov, Petar. *Baba Ega ili sbornik ot razlichni vyarvania, narodni lekuvania, magii, bayania i obichai v Kyustendilsko.* Tarnovo, 1887.]

Маринов, Димитър. *Избрани произведения в 5 тома. Том I, част 1.* Народна вяра. Изток-запад, София, 2003. [Marinov, Dimitar. *Izbrani proizvedenia v 5 toma. Tom I, chast 1. Narodna vyara.* Iztok-zapad, Sofia, 2003.]

Mierzwicki, Tony. *Hellenismos: Practicing Greek Polytheism Today.* Llewellyn Publications, 2018.

Mishev, Georgi. *Thracian Magic: Past & Present.* Avalonia Publishing, 2012.

Попов, Александър. "Баяния (басни) за урочасване." *Сборник за народни умотворения, наука и книжнина,* book I, 1889, pp. 78–79. [Popov, Aleksandar. "Bayania (basni) za urochasvane." *Sbornik za narodni umotvorenia, nauka i knizhnina,* book I, 1889, pp. 78–79.]

Сталийски, Цано. "Делба на светците и наказание на безверниците." *Сборник за народни умотворения, наука и книжнина,* book X, 1894, pp. 24–25. [Staliyski, Tsano. "Delba na svettsite i nakazanie na bezvernitsite." *Sbornik za narodni umotvorenia, nauka i knizhnina,* book X, 1894, pp. 24–25.]

Тодорова-Пиргова, Ивета. *Баяния и магии.* АИ "Проф. Марин Дринов", София, 2003. [Todorova-Pirgova, Iveta. *Bayania i Magii.* AI "Prof. Marin Drinov", Sofia, 2003.]

Йорова, Стефана. *Самодивата в българския фолклор.* Лени–АН, 2024. [Yorova, Stefana. *Samodivata v balgarskia folklor.* Leni–AN, 2024.]

Gentlidecht

Rejoicing at What We Have, Not Lamenting What We Lost

by P. Sufenas Virius Lupus

Since 2006, I have used the term "Gentlidecht" to identify the particular form of reconstructed Irish Polytheistic religious practice that I have followed since I first began my Polytheistic spiritual explorations and involvements in 1992.

Though I have been involved both formally and informally with what has been called "Celtic Reconstructionism" over the past several decades, and though I do have practices and devotional commitments with Deities, Heroes/Heroines, and other Divine Beings from a variety of Celtic cultures (as well as others),[1] I find "Celtic" to be a notoriously slippery term. It is often used in non-mainstream religio-spiritual circles to imprecisely describe the phenomena to which the term becomes attached. Not everything that is Irish or is found in Irish culture (ancient, medieval, and modern) is "Celtic." Nor are theoret-

1 For all such Beings—no matter the religions from which They originate—including all Deities, Spirits, Ancestors, and Elevated Humans (Heroes, Heroines, and Saints), both the general nouns referring to Them, as well as the pronouns used in relation to Them, are capitalized in the present discussion out of respect for Their divine qualities as a matter of my own devotional commitments.

ically "Common Celtic" linguistic or cultural formations actually found in exactly that form (or any form at all) within various periods of Irish culture. It would be deluded and whitewashed to call anything and everything Irish "Celtic" as it would be to call everything in popular culture and linguistic usage of the United States "Anglo-Saxon." This is the case in all periods of Irish culture, not simply because it was never entirely closed off to foreign influences of many types. Instead, the elements that distinguish Irish culture from Welsh, Gaulish, and other Celtic cultures originates from a complex interplay of factors beyond the different localizations of Christianity, the invasions of the Vikings, and colonization by Anglo- and Cambro- Norman in later medieval centuries. These factors include the indigenous, pre-Celtic layers of culture already in place from the Mesolithic period onwards, ongoing contact with what can be identified as Pictish culture and populations, and many others. The comparative philological, mythological, and cultural processes that illuminate Irish culture and place it within a wider context are useful and productive, but to subsume everything Irish into a fuzzy notion of the "Celtic" is as unhelpful as to call everything French "Romance," as if French is no different than Italian, Spanish, and Romanian. Though it may be (as one colorful medieval Irish text puts it) as useless as attempting to prevent a mare from farting, only using "Celtic" when it applies to a meta-level of linguistic and cultural comparison is always preferable. Also, when referring to cultures that are part of a wider set of complexes, it is both more intellectually honest as well as accurate to use the specific terms for a given culture (e.g. Irish, Scottish, Manx, Welsh, Breton, Cornish, Gaulish [Cisalpine or Transalpine], Galatian, Lepontic, Celtiberian, etc.).

But what is "Gentlidecht"?[2]

This question can be provisionally answered by examining a particular instance in which it is used in a medieval Irish text, the eleventh century *The Second Vision of Adomnán.* Because this is a Christian text,[3] what medieval Irish text is not at least influenced by Christianity?—it is not in the repertoire of many modern Irish Pagans and Polytheists in the same way that *Cath Maige Tuired,*[4]

---

2 I will capitalize this term, as well as all others referring to pre-modern and current religious movements (e.g. Paganism, Christianity, etc.), though I will leave it lower-case when it is given or quoted from medieval texts in which this respect is not given to it. When said texts are given in English translation, however, I will capitalize "Paganism" or "Heathenism" when these terms are used since, for our modern understandings, respect should be given to religions in our discourse (and translating these texts places them into our discourse!) no matter what the original discourse—polemical or otherwise—had to say about these phenomena.

3 Considering that narrative literature in Ireland was only possible through the literacy in Latin eventually applied to Irisih by Christian missionaries, what medieval Irish text isn't at least influenced by Christianity? While inscriptions in *ogam* (Old Irish; Modern Irish, ogham; though popular spirituality follows the Modern Irish form in its usage, I will use the Old Irish) might be considered an exception, even *ogam* is agreed at present to have arisen in contact with Latin literacy due to its similar separation of vowels and consonants, its number of vowels being the same as Latin, and a variety of other pieces of evidence which demonstrate these relationships definitively (McManus).

4 Gray

Táin Bó Cúailnge,[5] *Acallam na Senórach*,[6] *Lebor Gabála Érenn*,[7] and the *Ogam Tract* in *Auraicept na nÉces* from the *Book of Ballymote*,[8] amongst others, might be (at least in translation). While part of the reason for this is due to academic inaccessibility, there is an inbuilt bias within many modern Pagans and Polytheists to be angry at Christianity (with good reason!) for both historical and personal reasons. There is also an assumption that anything "polluted" with Christian influence is somehow less "pure" than unadulterated pre-Christian traditions. In actuality, what slips by the filters of medieval Irish Christian authors in discussing ostensibly Christian topics can be very valuable in learning about non-Christian forms of medieval Irish culture.

Before contextualizing the text and extracting useful information, let us examine it in itself. The term "gentlidecht" and its translation into English are in bold so as to more easily see where and how it is being used in the excerpt.

> *Ar ro lensat fir Erenn in* ***gentlidecht*** *doridisi amal cétna bui ria cretem, riasiú tísed Pátraic, acht naro adairset ídlu namá. Ar buí éthech ⁊déigbriathar oc géntiu⁊ ní fhil indíu, ocus cech olc do-gnítis na génti do-gnither uli i tír nErenn isin amsirsea, acht na hadrat ídlu namá, acht chena do-gniat guin ⁊ gait ⁊ adaltras, ⁊ fingalu ⁊ duinorcain ⁊ esorcain chell ⁊ clerech, sáint ⁊ éthech ⁊ goéi ⁊ gúbreth*

5 O'Rahilly. There are further recensions of this text than the two listed, but Recension III is more difficult to access, and Recension IV has not been edited or translated in an accessible form at present. More easily-available translations of this text (which often incorporate sections from both principal recensions, plus other tales in some cases) can be found in Thomas Kinsella's The Tain and Ciaran Carson's The Tain.

6 Dooley and Roe

7 Macalister

8 Calder 270–313

⁊ *coscrad eclasi* ⁊ *Dé, draidecht* ⁊ ***géntlidecht***[9] ⁊ *sénairecht, auptha* ⁊ *elmasa* ⁊ *fídlanna.*

For the men of Ireland have followed ***Paganism*** *again as it was at first before the Faith, before Patrick came, except only that they have not worshipped idols. For there was a false oath and a good word amongst the Heathens and there is not today, and every evil which the Heathens used to commit, is committed by all in the land of Ireland at this time, except only that they do not worship idols. However they commit wounding and theft and adultery, and kinslaying and manslaughter and harrying churches and clerics, avarice and perjury and falsehood and false judgement and overthrowing of God's church, Druidry and* ***Paganism*** *and augury, spells and charms, and divination.*[10]

The term "gentlidecht" is used in this, and other, medieval Irish texts to mean "Paganism," and comes ultimately from the Latin *gentes,* "nations," from which the term "Gentile" comes. While many Celtic Reconstructionist groups have created Irish and other Celtic neologisms as names for their polytheistic practices, but this is a thoroughly medieval Irish word for what the Christians understood to be the Paganism of ancient and medieval Ireland, which was still going strong—or, perhaps, made a resurgence (if the reports in this eleventh century text are to be given credence)—after centuries of post-Patrician conversion. In an older

9 The original text, as given in the following footnote, has the acute accent on the first "e" in this instance, whereas earlier in the quote, and in other uses of the term in different texts, it does not. This type of variation is not unheard of in many manuscripts, and generally does not impact the translation of words like this, whereas *fer* (man) versus *fér* (grass) is another matter! The general form of *gentlidecht* is the unaccented one, and thus that is what I will use in this discussion, except where original texts indicate otherwise. However, see Whitley Stokes' translation for another possibility on why this vowel might have been lengthened.

10 Volmering 647–681

translation of this text by Whitley Stokes from 1891, the word is translated, rather amusingly from a modern Pagan perspective, "Heathenism" or "Heathenry."[11] Some who practice "Irish Heathenry," taking elements of both Irish and Norse/Germanic traditions either separately or in syncretism, have misread older (nineteenth and early twentieth century) English translations as referring to their own traditions directly by the medieval authors, but with a fuller understanding of the context in which such translations were provided, there is no barrier to incorporating certain elements of the insights gained from studying such usages into a dual-tradition practice, either.

The text of *The Second Vision of Adomnán* is pseudepigraphically attributed to the late seventh-/early eighth-century St. Adomnán of Iona. St. Adomnán was the ninth Abbot of the island monastery of Iona, founded by His relative, St. Colm Cille, around a century before Adomnán Himself was its Abbot. He was the great-great-great-great-great-great-grandson of Niall Noígiallach, "Niall of the Nine Hostages," the founder of the Uí Néill dynasty of the Irish High Kings of Tara, Who ruled the northern half of Ireland from the late fourth century through the early seventeenth century, with very few interruptions in Their rule. (Not only does Niall have descendants in numbers rivaling Genghis Khan, He was also the protagonist of the most well-known Irish tale in which the Sovereignty Goddess of Ireland comes to Him in a hideous form to test His fitness for the kingship. She then becomes beautiful once He successfully passes Her trial by having sex with Her.[12]) Adomnán wrote an extensive *Vita of Columba,*[13] the Latinized version of St. Colm Cille's name, around the year 697 CE. Adomnán also wrote a piece on holy places

11 Stokes 420–443. It's the same passage as in the previous footnote. In the middle of Volmering's translation, she uses "Heathen" to translate *génti* (usually *genti*), the Irish root (borrowed from the Latin *gentes*) from which *gentlidecht* is derived.

12 Stokes 172–207, 446

13 Anderson and Anderson; Sharpe

in Palestine, Alexandria, and Constantinople, *De Locis Sanctis,* which was based on the work of the Gaulish monastic pilgrim, Arculf,[14] and which Adomnán presented to Aldfrith, the King of Northumbria, in 598 CE.[15] A law-text that Adomnán promulgated, the *Cáin Adomnáin,* was one of the first legal documents to attempt the protection of women, children, and clerics as "innocents" (i.e. non-combatants), and His law was re-promulgated on a number of occasions in future centuries.[16] There is also an apocalyptic visionary text of the Christian afterlife that is attributed to Him, *Fís Adomnáin,* the (First) "Vision of Adomnán"[17] (thus explaining why the text excerpted above is the "Second Vision"), which dates from the tenth or eleventh century, and which is most certainly not a text that He wrote Himself. The text contains a variety of interesting things, including the lines that are reminiscent of a fragment of *The Chaldean Oracles.*[18] Adomnán was one of the most learned men of His day in Ireland and Britain, and the presence of a great deal of Christian apocrypha in Ireland (as well as classical texts)[19] indicates that it is very possible that some otherwise strange or obscure ancient

---

14 O'Loughlin 33–52

15 Bieler and Meehan

16 Ní Dhonnchadha 53–68

17 Carey 261–274

18 Adomnán was one of the most learned men of His day in Ireland. I hope to treat this possibility in a future study. For an edition gathering all fragments of *The Chaldean Oracles* that are known to exist, see Majercik, *The Chaldean Oracles: Text, Translation, and Commentary.*

19 McNamara

texts may well have made their way there in some form or other.[20] The study of medieval Irish literature can unexpectedly reveal a great deal about pre-Christian religion, but it may not always be pre-Christian Irish religion, for good or ill!

The *Second Vision of Adomnán* actually dates to c. 1096 CE and was written in the hopes of reforming the Irish population and bringing them more in line with the Church's ecclesiastical disciplines and morality. The writer expected that the Christian Apocalypse might occur due to beliefs surrounding Mog Ruith's role in the execution of John the Baptist.[21] Mog Ruith was a legendary and heroic Ancestor in Irish myth Who learned warrior (and possibly mantic) arts from Scáthach, the female tutor of Cú Chulainn, and learned magic from "Simon Magus,"[22] Who in Irish is called Simon Druí ("Simon the Druid"). Various Christians believed that before his baptism by St. Philip, he mastered all kinds of sorcery and magical practices among the Samaritans. He had also challenged St. Peter to sell him the power to transmit the gifts of the Holy Spirit, which made Simon Druí the fountain of all heresies and teacher of the mysteries in some alternative (or, as some have said "Gnostic") Christian sects. Mog Ruith, the Druid and son of an Irish sage and a British slave-girl, was believed to have been taught by all of the

---

20 Carey 75–96. This bombastic cosmological tour by the disembodied light-being, The Ever-New Tongue, Who is in reality St. Philip the Apostle, shows evidence of having access to information only found in Egyptian tombs in the *Amduat* text: see Carey, "The Sun's Night Journey: A Pharaonic Image in Medieval Ireland," pp. 14–34. Carey also produced a full edition of the *Corpus Christianorum Series; Apocrypha Hiberniae II, Apocalyptica 1: In Tenga Bithnua, The Ever-New Tongue,* in which he notes that potential influences from such apocryphal Christian texts as the *Pistis Sophia* might be present as well.

21 For some of Mog Ruith's adventures, see Carey, "An Old Irish Poem about Mug Ruith," pp. 113–134; Ó Duinn, *Forbhais Droma Dámhgháire: The Siege of Knocklong.*

22 Ferreiro; Litwa

Druids of Ireland, including Simon Druí—Mog Ruith was both sufficiently skilled in magic and steeped in heresy to have been interpreted by the medieval readers of these texts as the font of much error in the pre-Christian traditions of Ireland. Mog Ruith, therefore, was the only person bold enough (and, it would be implied, both malevolent enough, as well as ignorant enough) to cut the head off St. John the Baptist. For this singular act of wickedness, much evil and hardship would be loosed upon the people of Ireland, the land of Mog Ruith's birth. This is the apotheosis of the "Irish Catholic guilt" complex: placing the responsibility for the literal end of the world on the shoulders of one wicked Ancestor of the Irish.

Mog Ruith is in no way a historical person, and this series of events narrated is not remotely factual. It is a medieval Irish literary myth that some very clever and enterprising Irish monastics created using based on their extensive knowledge of both Christian canonical and apocryphal narrative traditions (as well as, likely, the work of early heresiologists), to connect their own honored Ancestors to the narratives of the Gospels, subsequent patristic tradition, and other venerable sources. Such a clever and innovative story had the force of doctrine, and of very real prophetic insight, given to it, despite its non-canonically Christian status. No matter what religion the Irish practiced, stories created their realities, and what may seem to the modern view as a "retcon" of more established traditions from the wider non-Irish world was no barrier to taking such novel narratives seriously.[23]

---

23 Bernhardt-House 45–60. See the important references for this article (omitted by the publishers) available online with the article itself at https://www.academia.edu/47508867/Interpretatio_Hibernica; see also the way in which Mary's conception of Jesus is reinterpreted in the Irish prose introduction to the Christian hymn from the Gospel of Luke, the *Magnificat*, in the Irish collection known as the *Liber Hymnorum*; *Bernhardt-House*, "Queer Conceptions and Calculations: Niall Frossach and the Easter Controversy," pp. 186–205.

Mog Ruith's daughter, Tlachtga, is an important figure for a number of modern Irish Druids, Pagans, and Polytheists in Her own right.[24] Much more could be said about Her, and about Mog Ruith and wider Irish traditions connected with each, but in the context of *The Second Vision of Adomnán* and our understanding of the term "gentlidecht", the most important matters have been established. It was believed that, as a result of St. John the Baptist's beheading by Mog Ruith, when the feast of the Baptist's decollation fell on a Friday, as well as being accompanied by a number of other signs, it would signify the imminent eschaton;[25] such a configuration of dates then occurred in 1096 when *The Second Vision of Adomnán* was written. The writers hoped that a dedication to penance and a more secure conversion away from "Gentile" (which is a more literal and etymologically-transparent, rendering of Gentlidecht) practices would avert this world-ending scenario. Since almost 930 years have elapsed since that time, either the Irish calculation was incorrect (as has been every other prediction of the Christian eschaton, ancient or modern, including those of Jesus Himself!), or the efforts of the medieval Irish churchmen at promoting penitence and stemming apostasy were successful (possible, but not likely!). No matter what the reality is, this does demonstrate that even under the Christian dispensation, the Irish felt they could bargain with and even compel the will of their particular monotheistic Deity under certain circumstances, as occurs in many texts in which Saints and others "fast against" the Christian God in an echo of parts of the Old Irish legal process known as distraint (*athgabáil*) to have their grievances heard by those more powerful and elevated on the social hierarchy than them.[26]

---

24 Gwynn 186–191

25 O'Leary 51–60

26 For more on this process, see Binchy, "Distraint in Irish Law," pp. 22–77. This practice has continued to recent times in the hunger strikes at various points during twentieth century Irish history; Sweeney, "Irish Hunger Strikes and the Cult of Self-Sacrifice," pp. 421–437.

In medieval Irish texts, Gentlidecht is understood as referring to the pre-Christian religion of Ireland systematically. As *The Second Vision of Adomnán* also elaborates upon this term, providing insight into the features of Gentildecht, it becomes easier to reconstruct what was done in earlier periods. This allows us to look at the evidence of what actually survived. It guides us away from an imagined "Celtic" past, an Indo-European restoration, or any number of other methodologically questionable ideas or theories (even when appealing). It requires taking what the actual sources say more seriously, and finding out what the evidence indicates, rather than theorizing on what might have been, or mourning what has been lost (which often involves no small amount of fantasizing about what "should" have existed but may never have occurred in historical reality to or for anyone).

Some of the characteristics in *The Second Vision of Adomnán* can be discounted, either as mostly anachronistic (e.g. "harrying churches and clerics" and "overthrowing of God's church," although there may be more to say on this) or wishful thinking on the medieval ecclesiastical writers' part. Idolatry is mentioned twice, but it is said that this does not still occur in the textual present of the eleventh century. While there are certainly iconographic representations known in pre-Christian Irish archaeology (though the religious usage or significance of many of these is not certain), it is likely that this account has more to do with the authors' familiarity with narratives in the hagiographical accounts of figures like St. Patrick, which feature Him facing off against idolaters sacrificing to Crom Cruaich,[27] for example. Likewise, the list of sins and offenses included, as Volmering notes in this passage, corresponds closely to a list of sins given in the Old Irish table of penitential commutations.[28]

The anachronism of the pre-Christian period in Ireland, described as a time in which "harrying churches and clerics" took

27 Balé 87–101

28 Volmering 677, 129. For the penitential table, see Bieler, *The Irish Penitentials*, pp. 278.

place, which were occurring in the eleventh century temporal context, appears inconsistent, as it would have been impossible for there to be churches and clerics to harry if the religion which has those functionaries and structures had not come into Ireland. While it is possible that this could have referred to a time in which missionaries in Ireland were the minority and Christianity had not been firmly established, there may be a more interesting possibility as to why this idea is being expressed in this manner. The question of what class of person specifically would enact this kind of destruction may be the more crucial one, and the activities of a particular type of person in the non-Christian Irish society is identified consistently: the (usually) youthful hunter-warrior outcasts that were the first line of defense of a given tribe, which were known in heroic literature as the warriors of the *fíanna,* the *fénnidi,*[29] the roving and reaving *díberga,* and as *láech* (originating from the Latin *laicus,* originally meaning "layperson"), as well as a variety of related and other terms.[30] If these sorts of destruction were enacted, then the activities of these hunter-warrior outlaws indicates that the practices involved contact with (and, most often, protection from) supernatural entities and had a religious context within the Polytheistic and Animistic worldview prevailing in Ireland before Christianity. Thus, continuation of such practices (in sources where they can be identified), as well as recreations of these roles as spiritual protectors of communities—and, when necessary, first-line defenders against and harriers of those who would seek to suppress such practices—in the context of a modern understanding of Gentlidecht is also consistent with the sources as they are available to us. The anachronism of these descriptions of church-condemned

29 The best discussion of these phenomena, as well as of the most famous leader and member of a fían-band, Finn mac Cumhaill, is Nagy, *The Wisdom of the Outlaw: The Boyhood Deeds of Finn in Gaelic Narrative Tradition.*

30 See, for example, Sharpe, "Hiberno-Latin *Laicus,* Irish *Láech* and the Devil's Men," pp. 75–92; McCone, "Werewolves, Cyclopes, *Díberga* and *Fíanna:* Juvenile Delinquency in Early Ireland," pp. 1–22.

activities in this passage, therefore, attests to a path of sacred warrior disciplines being part of the pre-Christian religion of Ireland.

However, what of the crucial final phrases, which indicate specific practices more directly? These are *draidecht ⁊ géntlidecht ⁊ sénairecht, auptha ⁊ felmasa ⁊ fídlanna*, "druidry and Paganism and augury, spells and charms, and divination." Though each are complex matters, some earlier work, both by myself as well as other scholars, can provide insight into the possibilities of several of these.

While many are familiar with modern forms of Druidism or Druidry, the "druidry" referred to here (despite being given in a list along with Géntlidecht) does not refer to the religious edifice we have come to understand as ancient or modern Druidry, but instead to magical practice in general. We have seen above that Simon Magus's name and common epithet are regularly rendered into Irish as Simon Druí, "Simon the Druid," and throughout Irish texts, the Latin *magus* is translated as *druí,* plural *druïd* or *druïdi,* "druid."[31] Thus, what such "druids" do, *draidecht,* should be understood more as "magic" than as the ancient Gaulish or modern Welsh, Irish, and Pagan/Polytheist forms of cultural or religious Druidry. The evidence for magical practice in Irish texts is extensive, and not only includes accounts of various Druids (including Mog Ruith)[32] and others performing such operations, but also spoken incantations

31 McKenna 66–74; Lupus 6–26

32 Ó Duinn

and the gestures which accompany them.[33]

Let us examine the last of the items: *fidlanna.*[34] Since Stokes's late nineteenth century translation of *The Second Vision of Adomnán,* this term has been translated "divination," though how exactly this has been determined is complex. The term is a combination of *fid,* "wood," and *lann,* a "thin plate" or "blade." The term appears again in *Imacallam in Dá Thuarad* ("The Colloquy of the Two Sages"), a text of perhaps the ninth century CE (but its earliest version is found in the twelfth century manuscript known as the *Book of Leinster*), comes in a line of obscurantist riddling dialogue: *techait fidlaind,* which Stokes translates as "wooden blades flee."[35] A gloss on this line reads *.i. tiagait ass na lanna co fi, .i. in gentlecht,* which Stokes translates as "i.e. the blades with poison depart, i.e. the heathenism (magic)," with the word "gentlecht" similarly to Gentlidecht, and then adds in his note, "Were they divining rods? or planchettes?" and gives a reference back to his text's edition and glossary for *The Second Vision of Adomnán.*[36] Something along the lines of "divination with wood" seems possible, and thus many modern Druids, Pagans, and Polytheists might conclude that this is a reference to divinatory usage of *ogam.* While this isn't certain, there is an Irish medieval

---

33 See Borsje, "Druids, Deer and 'Words of Power': Coming to Terms with Evil in Medieval Ireland," pp. 122–149; Borsje, "A Spell Called Éle," pp. 193-212; Borsje, "Celtic Spells and Counterspells,", pp. 9–50; Mees, *Celtic Curses;* Bernhardt-House, "Magic and Narrative: Ulster Cycle Texts as Historiolae," pp. 213–220; Carey, *Magic, Metallurgy & Imagination in Medieval Ireland: Three Studies,* particularly the first chapter, "Magical Texts in Early Medieval Ireland," pp. 1–28; and Carey, *King of Mysteries,* pp. 127–138. This is only a selective sample of some of the more recent scholarship currently available on this relatively small corpus of texts, which have yet to receive proper editions in nearly all cases.

34 Lupus 69–73. A reduced synopsis with some references, plus a further possibility on this, is given here.

35 Stokes 4–64

36 Stokes 33

tale that attributes the creation of the first ogam to Ogma, who used a knife to inscribe the first ogam on wood. Just as Ogma is the father of ogam, Ogma's knife is its mother. Intriguingly, lann can also mean "blade."

There is also a frequent occurrence within Irish texts of renowned bladed instruments and swords, capable of speaking, either through the intervention of demons living in them, or via *ogam* inscribed on or in the hilt (which would have often been wood).[37] If the "wood-blade" combination referred to a wooden-hilted sword with inscribed *ogam* used for divinatory or spiritual purposes (like allowing swords to speak), this might be a potential meaning of the term as well.

Sénairecht as "augury" does not present very much difficulty: it is the work of a *sénaire,* a diviner or enchanter, who is more literally a "reader-of-signs," which its root *sén* means, deriving from the Latin *signum,* "sign/portent/omen." The term *auptha* comes from the Old Irish *epaid,* and means "spell/charm" in a manner that can be positive or negative, comparable to the Greek term φάρμακον (*pharmakon,* "remedy" or "poison").[38] The term *felmasa* is further understood as "enchantment/spell," in one seventeenth century Irish glossary by the antiquary and chronicler Mícheál Ó Cléirigh, it is defined as "evil knowledge" (*droichfhios*).[39]

It may seem odd that the long-e version of Gentlidecht is found amidst *draidecht,* "magic," and *sénairecht,* another word defined as "magic," which is how it has been understood by contemporary translators. However, if the form "géntlidecht" is not an error nor a mere variation, the long-e may reveal something even more interesting. Such a lengthened vowel can be the result of the linguistic process of lengthening stemming from the loss of consonants or syllables in subsequent parts of a word. It has been assumed that the basis of Gentlidecht is the Old Irish word *genti,* "Gentile,"

37 Borsje 224–248; Bernhardt-House 5–19

38 Borsje 172–190

39 Miller 349–428

but also "Heathens/Pagans" and "magical." There is another word in Old Irish that is orthographically close to *genti,* which is *genit* (or occasionally *geinit*), plural *geniti,* often used in the phrase *geniti glinne,* "spirits of the glen." The meaning given in the Dictionary of the Irish Language is the rather circuitous "female mythical being of malevolent powers,"[40] or in the case of being ascribed in some instances to the Hero Cú Chulainn, "a weird, sprite-like creature."[41]

Liam Breatnach connects this term to several others in Welsh and Gaulish, and concludes that the ultimate origin for the term is similar to the Old Irish *geined,* "someone or something created/ brought into being; offspring, person, creation."[42] In this, Breatnach departs from earlier etymologies which suggested a connection with the Old Irish *gen,* "smile/laugh," and yet, this latter term may also have its role to play. One of the three types of music understood to be important for Irish skilled harpers is the *gentraige,* the "laughing strain," which magically causes those who hear it to laugh (along with the other two, *goltraige* and *súantrige,* the "crying strain" and the "sleeping strain" respectively), and thus *gentraige* also becomes associated with magic in general, along with Gentlidecht.

One wonders if, like the Genius Loci of Latin tradition, and like Genii (of individual humans, the Genius Augusti, and so forth) more

---

40 *(Dictionary of the Irish Language, based mainly on Old and Middle Irish Materials, Compact Edition).* (See also the fully updated online version of this, *An Electronic Dictionary of the Irish Language,* based on the *Contributions to a Dictionary of the Irish Language,* https://dil.ie/.)

41 It is to be noted that this modern lexical distinction attempts to draw a dividing line between a Feminine Spiritual Being and the great Irish Hero, when in reality Cú Chulainn remains highly ambiguous in gendered characteristics at best, and might even be understood usefully as either non-binary or even trans in certain cases.

42 Breatnach 195-196

widely and in general, the *geniti* were originally, and more simply, Spirits-of-Place, especially since *geniti* tends to occur so often along with *glenn,* genitive *glinne,* a specific geographic term. Perhaps, if there was a term involving specific interaction with various forms of *geniti,* and *geniti glinne* specifically, such a term might have originally been *genitidecht,*[43] and then this term became *géntidecht* when the quadrisyllabic term became trisyllabic, with compensatory lengthening of the "e" as a result. Later, this term may have eventually fallen together with Gentlidecht under "non-Christian/Gentile magical and religious practices generally," and became indistinguishable from it in its generalized maligned magical valence.

The similarity of the terms and the particularities of linguistic change could have easily lead to a synonymizing of the terms, and a simple lack of taking proper notice on the part of modern scholars to account for such a variation (though, admittedly, a minor one) could obscure the fact that the first three terms in the list were all intended to map onto a set of distinctions found elsewhere in medieval Europe quite widely when it comes to magic:[44] "natural

---

43 One wonders if this might be a phenomenon akin to what the Ancient Greeks referred to as Nympholepsy, the "seizing" of a person by sudden poetic inspiration or other forms of mantic frenzy, but also the deliberate cultivation of relationships with Nymphs (Who were generally tied to specific geographic locations) by particular individuals who often set themselves up in caves that Nymphs haunted; see Connor, "Seized by the Nymphs: Nympholepsy and Symbolic Expression in Classical Greece," pp.155–189; Larson, *Greek Nymphs: Myth, Cult, Lore*; Pache, *A Moment's Ornament: The Poetics of Nympholepsy in Ancient Greece.* It would be an interesting way to understand the relationship between the Sovereignty Goddesses and Irish Kings as a kind of "regional/national Nympholepsy," taken to a heightened degree!

44 E.g., Walker, *Spiritual and Demonic Magic: From Ficino to Campanella.*

magic," perhaps applying here to *druidecht*,[45] which often does feature manipulation of the elements and other natural characteristics of the material cosmos; "demonic magic," understood to involve the summoning and interaction with non-corporeal non-Christian Entities (thus, *geniti glinne* easily become understood as "Demons" by some), and thus applying to *géntlidecht*; and "divination/omen-reading/augury," *sénairecht*. This accented form of *géntlidecht* may then not be pre-Christian magic and/or religion generally, but rather a specific form of spiritwork involving Land Spirits of various types... indeed, a truly Gentile, Heathen, and Pagan practice in the literal sense of each!

Of course, there is far more of use that can be found in medieval Irish literature that can be fairly easily operationalized in a modern magical and/or religious practice for Druids, Pagans, Polytheists, and magicians and occultists more widely, which is not covered in this passage from *The Second Vision of Adomnán*. The strong tradition of toponymy and topographical lore, known in Irish as Dindshenchas, "Lore of Famous/Sacred Places," runs throughout Irish literature, and adopting such understandings of

---

45 Though the original text has *draidecht*, these two variations are often found in Old Irish texts, and before now have not been differentiated in meaning. Broad vowels like "a" and "u" can often interchange easily in medieval Irish texts, even within a single text on a given manuscript page. This debate continues into the modern period, and is even visible in how Stokes wrote "Adamnan" in his edition and translation of the late 1800s, the Andersons rendered His name as "Adomnan" in the 1960s when they first produced their translation of *Vita Columbae*, and modern scholars from the 1980s and 1990s onward have preferred the standardized form to be "Adomnán."

the "genealogy of place"[46] can be an excellent basis for Gentlidecht (and *géntlidecht!*) no matter where one lives. In addition to magical texts and occasional ritual directions, there are also various gnomic texts which can instruct on ethics as well.[47] Old Irish laws were very detailed in how they described the responsibilities and requirements of various social roles, and the duties and expectations for those who hold them. Amongst the most detailed are those involving poets (*fili,* plural *filid*) and the practice of Filidecht, which involves a good amount of magical and supernatural activity, knowledge, and, of course, dialogue with Spiritual Beings.[48] There are even some sources that contain what might be hymnody to particular groups of Deities and Their spiritual servants,[49] or the texts which have been transmitted can serve that function very easily in the present if they did not do so in the past. It becomes clear that a great deal of impact can be readily enacted based directly on surviving medieval

---

46 I thank Dr. A. Joseph McMullen for this memorable and powerful phrase; I wish he would put it into print somewhere! For some of the Dindshenchas (in addition to Gwynn), see Whitley Stokes, "The Prose Tales in the Rennes Dindshenchas," vol. 15, pp. 272–336, 418–484; vol. 16, pp. 31–83, 135–167, 269–312.

47 E.g. Fomin, "Bríatharthecosc Con Culainn in the Context of Early Irish Wisdom Literature," pp. 140–172.

48 Modern movements in this direction include Laurie, *Ogam: Weaving Word Wisdom.*

49 Specifically: Brian, Iuchar, and Iucharba, the Three Gods of Skill *(Tri Dée Dána),* also known as the Sons of Tuirill Bicreo (or Tuireann, or other variations), Who are described as the sons of Brigit the Poetess (note: a singular Brigit that is poet, smith, and leech is not attested in medieval Irish texts, and this notion only comes from a modern scholarly oversimplification, as well as the popular spiritual conflation—and both as the result of unexamined monotheizing biases—of these three Goddesses with St. Brigid of Kildare, and other Saints called Brigid and relatively unrelated Heroines called Brig, which deserves its own discussion!) in the text edited by Carey, "A Tuath Dé Miscellany," pp. 24–45.

Irish sources, and while some things are certainly lost or incomplete, what does survive is a feast, a treasure trove, and a blessing for those who have the desire to look for it, the knowledge to access it and the wisdom to discern what is best in it—whether it is from the strains of Irish cultural tradition that have survived, or is from a hibernicization of Christian, Classical Greek, Roman, and other sources that the medieval Irish read, interpreted, redefined, and assimilated as their own.[50]

What can be known of Irish Polytheism from the medieval sources which have survived: that is Gentlidecht.

May the Gods and the Non-Gods smile upon
those who come to know these ways
with victory, blessings, good hospitality,
and health for all their days!

---

50 We should understand that both theological and methodological syncretism is not—as has often been said by monotheistic anti-syncretists—either sinful or impure, neither are these pollutions of tradition, symptoms of systems or worldviews in decline, nor poor attempts at monotheizing and universalism, but instead the default mode of human religions the world over in every time period, save for those that attempt (and inevitably fail!) to police their boundaries so stringently as to eliminate what they are able to identify as "other" elements, while generally failing to recognize what elements they have retained that are derived from earlier or later external traditions (generally to positive results!). For more on better and more productive views of syncretism for modern Polytheists, Pagans, and anyone else interested, see Lupus, *A Serpent Path Primer*, pp. 1–61.

Bibliography

Anderson, Alan Orr and Marjorie Ogilvie Anderson, translator. *Adomnan's Life of Columba.* Oxford University Press, 1991.

Balé, Marcos A. "Sacrifice at Samain: The Figure of Crom Cruaich." *Cosmos: The Yearbook of the Traditional Cosmology Society*, vol. 18, 2002, pp. 87–101.

Bernhardt-House, Phillip A. "Interpretatio Hibernica." *Eolas: Journal of the American Society of Irish Medieval Studies*, vol. 2, 2007, pp. 45–60.

—. "Magic and Narrative: Ulster Cycle Texts as *Historiolae*." *Ulidia 3*, pp. 213–220.

—. "Queer Conceptions and Calculations: Niall Frossach and the Easter Controversy." *Canadian Journal of Irish Studies/ Revue Canadienne d'*Études *Irlandaises*, vol. 39.1, 2015, pp. 186–205.

—. "Warriors, Words, and Wood: Oral and Literary Wisdom in the Exploits of Irish Mythological Warriors." *Studia Celtic Fennica*, vol. 6, 2009, pp. 5–19.

Bieler, Ludwig, translator. *The Irish Penitentials.* Dublin Institute for Advanced Studies, 1963, p. 278.

—and Denis Meehan. *Adamnan's De Locis Sanctis.* Dublin Institute for Advanced Studies, 1958.

Binchy, Daniel A. "Distraint in Irish Law." *Celtica*, vol. 10, 1973, pp. 22–77.

Borsje, Jacqueline. "Celtic Spells and Counterspells." *Understanding Celtic Religion: Revisiting the Pagan Past*, University of Wales Press, 2015, pp. 9-50.

—. "Druids, Deer and 'Words of Power': Coming to Terms with Evil in Medieval Ireland." *Approaches to Religion and Mythology in Celtic Studies*, Cambridge Scholars Publishing, 2008, pp. 122–149.

—. "A Spell Called Éle." *Ulidia 3: Proceedings of the Third International Conference on the Ulster Cycle of Tales, University of Ulster, Coleraine, 22-25 June, 2009*, Curach Bhán Publications, 2013, pp. 193–212.

—. "Omens, Ordeals, and Oracles: On Demons and Weapons in Early Irish Texts." *Peritia,* vol. 13, 1999, pp. 224-248.

—. "Rules & Legislation on Love Charms in Early Medieval Ireland" *Peritia,* vol. 21, 2010, pp. 172-190.

Breatnach, Liam. "Varia II: 1. Irish *geined* and *geinit,* Gaulish *geneta,* Welsh *geneth,*" *Ériu,* vol. 45, 1994, pp. 195-196.

Calder, George, translator. *Auraicept na n-Éces: The Scholar's Primer.* Four Courts Press, 1995, pp. 270–313.

Carey, John. *Apocrypha Hiberniae II, Apocalyptica 1: In Tenga Bithnua, The Ever-New Tongue.* Brepols, 2009.

—. "A Tuath Dé Miscellany." Bulletin of the Board of Celtic Studies, vol. 39, 1992, pp. 24–45.

—, translator. *King of Mysteries: Early Irish Religious Writings.* Four Courts Press, 2000, pp. 75–96, 127–138, 261–274.

—. *Magic, Metallurgy & Imagination in Medieval Ireland: Three Studies.* Celtic Studies Publications, 2019, pp. 1–28.

—. "An Old Irish Poem about Mug Ruith." *Journal of the Cork Historical and Archaeological Society,* vol. 110, 2005, pp. 113–134.

—. "The Sun's Night Journey: A Pharaonic Image in Medieval Ireland." *Journal of the Warburg and Courtauld Institutes,* vol. 57, 1994, pp. 14–34.

Carson, Ciaran, translator. *The Tain.* Penguin, 2009.

Connor, W. R. "Seized by the Nymphs: Nympholepsy and Symbolic Expression in Classical Greece." *Classical Antiquity,* vol. 7.2, 1988, pp. 155–189.

Dictionary of the Irish Language, based mainly on Old and Middle Irish Materials, Compact Edition. Royal Irish Academy, 1983.

Dooley, Ann and Harry Roe, translator. *Tales of the Elders of Ireland: Acallam na Senórach.* Oxford University Press, 1999.

Ferreiro, Alberto. *Simon Magus in Patristic, Medieval and Early Modern Traditions.* Brill, 2005.

Fomin, Maxim. "Bríatharthecosc Con Culainn in the Context of Early Irish Wisdom Literature." *Ulidia 2: Proceedings of the Second International Conference on the Ulster Cycle of Tales, Maynooth, 24-27 June, 2005,* An Sagart, 2009, pp. 140–172.

Gray, Elizabeth, translator. *Cath Maige Tuired: The Second Battle of Maige Tuired.* Irish Texts Society, 1982.McManus, Damian. *A Guide to Ogam.* Maynooth: An Sagart, 1991.

Gwynn, Edward, translator. *The Metrical Dindshenchas.* Dublin Institute for Advanced Studies, 1991, vol. 4, pp. 186–191.

Kinsella, Thomas, translator. *The Tain.* Oxford University Press, 1969.

Larson, Jennifer. *Greek Nymphs: Myth, Cult, Lore.* Oxford University Press, 2001.

Laurie, Erynn Rowan. *Ogam: Weaving Word Wisdom.* Immanion/Megalithica, 2007.

Litwa, David. *Simon Magus? The Sources and Stories of Christianity's First Archenemy.* M. David Litwa, 2024.

—. *Simon of Samaria and the Simonians: Contours of an Early Christian Movement.* Bloomsbury/T&T Clark, 2024.

Lupus, P. Sufenas Virius. "*Fidlanna* in Old Irish." *Walking the Worlds ("Divination and Oracles"),* vol. 3.2, 2017, pp. 69–73.

—. "The Irish *Druí* as Magicians Rather Than [Gaulish] 'Druids.'" *Walking the Worlds ("Magic and Religion"),* vol. 2.1, 2015, pp. 6–26.

—. *A Serpent Path Primer.* The Red Lotus Library, 2016, pp. 1–61.

Macalister, Robert Alexander Stewart. *Lebor Gabála Érenn, The Book of the Taking of Ireland.* Vol. 1-5, 1956.

Majerick, Ruth, translator. *The Chaldean Oracles: Text, Translation, and Commentary.* Brill, 1989.

McCone, Kim. "Werewolves, Cyclopes, *Díberga* and *Fíanna*: Juvenile Delinquency in Early Ireland." *Cambridge Medieval Celtic Studies,* vol. 12, 1986, pp. 1–22.

McKenna, Catherine. "Between Two Worlds: Saint Brigit and Pre-Christian Religion in the *Vita Prima,*" *CSANA Yearbook 2: Identifying the 'Celtic,'* Four Courts Press, 2002, pp. 66–74.

McNamara, Martin. *The Apocrypha in the Irish Church.* Dublin Institute for Advanced Studies, 1975.

Mees, Bernard. *Celtic Curses.* The Boydell Press, 2009.

Miller, Arthur W. K., translator. "O'Clery's Irish Glossary." *Revue Celtique,* vol. 4, 1880, pp. 349–428.

Nagy, Joseph F. *The Wisdom of the Outlaw: The Boyhood Deeds of Finn in Gaelic Narrative Tradition.* University of California Press, 1985.

Ní Dhonnchadha, Máirín, translator. "The Law of Adomnán: A Translation." *Adomnán at Birr, AD 697: Essays in Commemoration of the Law of the Innocents,* Four Courts Press, 2001, pp. 53–68.

Ó Duinn, Seán. *Forbhais Droma Dámhgháire: The Siege of Knocklong.* Mercier Press, 1992.

O'Leary, Aideen M. "Mog Ruith and Apocalypticism in Eleventh-Century Ireland." *The Individual in Celtic Literatures, Celtic Studies Association of North America Yearbook 1,* Four Courts Press, 2001, pp. 51–60.

O'Loughlin, Thomas. "The Library of Iona in the Late Seventh Century: The Evidence from Adomnán's *De Locis Sanctis.*" *Ériu,* vol. 45, 1994, pp. 33–52.

O'Rahilly, Cecile, translator. *Táin Bó Cúailnge, Recension I.* Dublin Institute for Advanced Studies, 1967.

—. *Táin Bó Cúailnge from the Book of Leinster.* Dublin Institute for Advanced Studies, 1968.

Pache, Corinne Ondine. *A Moment's Ornament: The Poetics of Nympholepsy in Ancient Greece.* Oxford University Press, 2010.

Sharpe, Richard, translator. *Adomnán of Iona: Life of St. Columba.* Penguin, 1995.

—. "Hiberno-Latin *Laicus*, Irish *Láech* and the Devil's Men," *Ériu,* vol. 30, 1979, pp. 75–92.

Stokes, Whitley. "Adamnan's Second Vision." *Revue Celtique,* vol. 12, 1891, sec. 15–16, pp. 420–443.

—. "The Colloquy of the Two Sages." *Revue Celtique,* vol. 26, 1905, sec. 153, pp. 4–64.

—, translator. "The Death of Crimthann Son of Fidach, and the Adventures of the Sons of Eochaid Muigmedón." *Revue Celtique,* vol. 24, 1903, pp. 172–207, 446.

—. "The Prose Tales in the Rennes Dindshenchas." *Revue Celtique,* vol. 15, 1894, pp. 272–336, 418–484; vol. 16, 1895, pp. 31–83, 135–167, 269–312.

Sweeney, George. "Irish Hunger Strikes and the Cult of Self-Sacrifice." *Journal of Contemporary History,* vol. 28.3, 1993, pp. 421–437.

Volmering, Nicole. "The Second Vision of Adomnán." *The End and Beyond: Medieval Irish Eschatology*, Celtic Studies Publications, 2014, sec. 6, pp. 647–681.

Walker, D.P. *Spiritual and Demonic Magic: From Ficino to Campanella.* Penn State University Press, 2000.

The Power of Purification

A Finnish Folk Magic Primer

by Aili Marjatta Kerttula

Tervetuloa and welcome, esteemed readers. Sit down by the woodstove for a while so I can weave you a tale. Have a cup of coffee and some fresh *pulla* (sweet cardamom bread) and make yourself comfortable. I am so happy you're here. Your very presence in this space with me means that we are kindred; one of the same heart and spirit. I myself spent my entire life dreaming of finding this knowledge, and it gives me so much joy and honor to be able to pass what I have learned along to you.

Finland has long been something of a "lost" country; stuck like the proverbial monkey in the middle between the two martial powers of Sweden and Russia. Even in this modern day, Finnish and Baltic magic and paganism are suspiciously missing from the narratives around the magical history of Europe. Some scholars have suggested that the Finno-Ugric peoples may even be the "First People" to have inhabited Northern Europe, but still we remain strangely forgotten or ignored. This doesn't even account for the Sámi people living above the Arctic Circle in Northern Europe, north of Norway, Sweden, Finland, and parts of Russia. The Sámi are the only recognized indigenous peoples of Europe and most people haven't even heard of their name.

People still erroneously lump Finland's folklore into "Scandinavian" stories and myth, but Finland has its own unique, glittering gem of a magical tradition that is just waiting to be rediscovered. And now *you* are the treasure hunter poised to become the benefactor of this trove of knowledge and mystery.

Ancient Magic

First, let us go way back to the Stone Age. The Proto-Finns and Proto-Saami people likely lived in the same areas together during what is today called the "Comb Ceramic Period." This time period was so named because of the ceramic pots with parallel line etched designs on them that appeared to have been created using a comb or similar implement. Many of these archeological finds that have been discovered indicate a strong animistic, shamanistic culture with especially notable totemic ties to the bear spirit and the elk spirit. These finds include cave and rock paintings as well as ritual burial sites. Shamans from these cultures traveled to the spirit realm to heal community members, perform divination, engage in spiritual "battles" with neighboring village healers, and officiate meetings, weddings, and more. The word "shaman," it is worth noting here, is derived from the Siberian tribal culture, and is inspired by their specific word for the tradition of the village healer who has the ability to traverse the realms of Spirit. Many other cultures have their own titles for healers and magical practitioners like these, but the academic community latched on to the easily understood term "shaman" and began applying it universally to all similar traditions ever since. However, in Finland these figures were most commonly called *noita* or, later in the early modern period, *tietäjä*. These early forms of shamanism were the most foundational spiritual beliefs and systems of the Finnish peoples.

We know a decent amount about the ancient shamanic peoples who eventually settled in Finland through archaeology. However, most of the knowledge we have today about the unique magic of the Finnish people comes from folklore and ethnography collected during the late 1800s and early 1900s during a time often referred to as the Kalevala Era. If you're not familiar, the Kalevala is the Finnish national epic which is a collection of mythological poems in the same vein as the Icelandic and Norse sagas that were compiled and arranged by a man named Elias Lonnröt in the 1800s. The poems, or "runes" as they're frequently called, in the Kalevala are composites of poems and narratives that were collected by Lonnröt and many of his contemporaries in the eighteenth and nineteenth centuries. These poems came from the far reaches of the East and West of Finland where the old ways had not yet surrendered fully to the smothering grip of Christianity. With Finland and its sister province, Karelia, so far from the epicenters of spreading Christianity, it took much longer to fully succumb to the hostile takeover. So, by the time these runes were being written down for posterity, they had already been slowly molded and influenced by the Medieval Christian worldview for hundreds of years. However, in spite of that, there are still stunning glimmers of an ancient pagan tradition at the core of these runes and incantations that are utterly irrepressible and glaringly obvious to those with the magically attuned eyes to read them. Over history to date, the influence of paganism on Christianity and Christianity on paganism has become so enmeshed that I don't believe this influence should scare the potential practitioner away as the golden riches that lie beneath sparkle so brightly, they are hard to ignore once you spot them.

By this early modern period, the *tietäjä* (literally meaning "one who knows") had replaced the *noita* as the main spiritual leader for a community. (In fact, the *noita* became conflated with evil paganism, whereas the *tietäjä* often included elements of Christianity and was, therefore, considered much "safer" and "godly" by comparison.) The *tietäjä* differed from their primordial shamanic ancestors in that they also performed magic for community members in addition to many of the tasks listed above for the village shamanic healer. For example, they would do spells for those who felt their cattle had been cursed, to help those accused of crimes to escape the ire of the courts, to assure a good hunt, or to help a woman attract the right husband. A great part of this special magic of the *tietäjä* is in the magic of *syntyn;* runes that describe the origin of an elemental force, animal, or illness/disease. Within this distinctly Finnish system, it was believed that if you knew the origin of a thing it gave you power over it. By reciting these runes, you could cure the ill, staunch blood, heal burns, prevent frostbite, ward off farmyard pests, or restore a person's *luonto* (personal power) when it was lost by fright or trauma. In modern neo-shamanism, this is often referred to as "soul loss."

The Power of the Tietäjä

Luonto was of prime importance to the *tietäjä* as it represents one's innate magical ability to affect change; affect change and successfully cast spells. *Luonto* could be raised to increase its potency through ritual or incantation, but in its latent form was often described as either "hard" or "soft." It was believed that in order for a practitioner to be a successful *tietäjä* one had to be born with a "hard" *luonto.* A particularly interesting piece of folklore suggests that people who are born with teeth nearly always have hard *luonto,* but the complement to that was that when elderly practitioners lost their teeth, their *luonto* was said to be lessened.

In addition to increasing the effectiveness of one's magic, having hard *luonto* was also believed to be able to protect the practitioner or individual from magical curses or attacks. Prior to or part of every ritual, spell, or healing work, the *tietäjä* would include *luonto*-raising. According to some ethnographies, this was done by gnashing the teeth together, jumping up and down, clapping the hands, spitting, coughing, or being angry. The *luonto* was sometimes summoned from under the ground through incantations if it seemed that these techniques were not sufficient. It is interesting to also acknowledge that these were likely techniques for inducing altered states of consciousness similar to the those used by the Ivank shamans in Siberia.

Commonly, in literature, *tietäjä* are referred to as being male and having hard *luonto.* Thus, having this "hard" *luonto* associated that characteristic with masculinity and virility. In fact, it was explicitly described in one account that, "a woman cannot manage to control any kind of *väki* [nature spirits/forces]" and female *tietäjä* were often characterized in narratives as having secondary male features such as facial hair to help explain their otherwise unusual competency with magic. That said, there certainly were recorded instances of female *tietäjä* and healers, but they were considered the exception rather than the norm.

However, there is emerging evidence for women having their own form of personal power called *lempi* or *vitun-väki*. At the surface *lempi*, as a term, is most commonly applied to a woman's marriage-ability, fertility, or sexual attractiveness. The word *lempi* is also comparable to the terms *kunnia* or *auvo*, which mean honor, value, or worth, and are synonymous with *lempi* in the Kalevala and many incantations. It bears mentioning that in the time period in which the ethnographic accounts speaking on *lempi* were collected (late 1800–early 1900), women had very little personal agency and often their ability to marry into a wealthy family was their best chance for lifelong prosperity and security. *Lempi* symbolized a singular and exclusive pathway to what was hopefully happiness, success, and, if she was lucky, love in marriage.

Vitun-väki is a type of vital force that was believed to emanate from female genitalia. In the accounts given, this energy had the power both to create new life, protect someone from the influences of the evil eye, and curse or injure a person. In fact, having a woman step over you was believed to be enough to cast an unintentional curse on someone, according to at least one narrative account. Rituals and spells (most commonly in the sauna) would be performed before marriage, and again after birthing children to either "open" or "close" this proverbial portal of magical energy. Likewise, women who were unable to give birth were sometimes put through *vitun-väki*-opening rituals to help them conceive a child. There is even a connection for this vital feminine force to the sauna stove and elemental fire *tulen-väki* as it was believed that sitting too close to the stove could cause infertility. The proximity and exposure to elemental fire *tulen-väki* had a regulating effect on this power in small doses, but could be catastrophic with over-use. The connection to fire somehow seems incredibly appropriate in its own ability to both destroy but also help build new life.

Some scholars debate whether or not *lempi* and *vitun-väki,* and *tulen-väki* are connected and perhaps enmeshed energies related specifically to female spiritual powers. Knowing that the woman and the goddess were such prevalent and revered figures in Ancient Finnish culture, I believe these concepts are most certainly connected even though these are not ideas that have been widely studied or yet understood from an academic perspective. I imagine that *luonto* and *lempi/vitun-vaki* function similarly to the idea of *shiva* and *shakti* energy of Hindu thought. They are two sides of the same coin of personal power frequently associated with the binary gender system (but which, of course, can function outside of the gender-binary for modern practitioners as well).

Tietäjä regularly opened any ceremony or ritual by raising their *luonto. Lempi* and *vitun-väki* were historically "raised" or "opened" in different ways than *luonto;* typically through sauna bathing rituals or spells/incantations. However, for the modern practitioner, a simpler ritual could achieve the same goal if one feels the need to draw on or increase their own personal power for fortitude or strength.

Simple Luonto/Vitun-väki Raising Ritual

In this simple ritual, I've used the word "power" rather than *luonto, lempi,* or *vitun-väki,* but feel free to substitute those as you feel led to do.

Supplies:

- Water collected from a clean, natural source
- A candle/small fire
- An offering bowl & offering (an ideal offering is typically liquor, bread, beer, or silver/gold)

- Drum or rattle (optional)

Begin by washing your hands and face with the water for purification before beginning. As you do so, you may say,

ENGLISH:	FINNISH:
Water spirits, ancient power	*Veden henget, voima vanha,*
Flowing sweetly, magic hour	*Virtaa taika, hetki kanna*
Cleanse and heal me, purify,	*Puhdista ja paranna,*
Wash my spirit, clarify,	*Henki huuhdo, kirkasta.*
Wisdom, healing, never stray	*Viisaus ja voima kanna,*
Guide me now and light my way.	*Näytä tie ja mua johda.*

Take a few moments to breathe and allow yourself to become fully present in your body at this moment in time. When you feel ready, light the candle and prepare to make your offering. Gift the offering to the Spirits and say:

ENGLISH:	FINNISH:
Land of Spirits, hear my cry,	*Henkimaa, nyt huuto soi,*
Guardians of the Earth and Sky.	*Maan ja taivaan vartijat,*
Ancestors attend my plea,	*Esivanhemmat, kuulkaa nyt,*
Channel power back to me.	*Voiman virta, mulle sytyt.*
With this gift, your guard I seek,	*Tällä lahjall' suojan saan,*
Be with me, as magic speaks.	*Olkaa luonain loitsimaan.*

Once you've made your offering, it is time to start the chanting or singing. You may accompany yourself with a drum or rattle, if desired. Begin chanting slowly and softly and as you fall into a rhythm with the words, allow yourself to get louder and faster.

ENGLISH:	FINNISH:
Power reaching high above,	*Voima nousee korkealle,*
Flying freely, purest love.	*Rakkaus on puhdas, hälle.*
Harmony on Earth and Sky,	*Taivaan, maan tuo sopu vain,*
Heal me, whole and purified.	*Paranna ja puhdas ain'.*

As you do, visualize the flame of your personal power growing in your belly, getting bigger and brighter, consuming your whole body. When you feel as though the chant has worked, simply stop and add the final statement, "*Ja niin se on.*" ("And so it is.")

When you are done, take a moment to once again feel present in this place and time. When you feel balanced and ready, extinguish the candle and the ritual is complete.

Merging the Magical and Modern

The Ancient Finns were a very animistic culture and held a likewise animistic worldview. Animism implores us that when we are seeking to revive or reconstruct an old tradition there is great value in paying attention to the traditions and beliefs that have managed to cross the threshold of time into modernity. These evergreen traditions tend to be the most accessible to us as contemporary practitioners. They are also often the most relevant to the experience of living a modern life due to having evolved alongside popular culture. However, it is healthy and necessary to also recognize that the Christian near-conquering of pagan folkways has inextricably altered and impacted these ideologies and spiritual practices. We should strive to recognize and adopt a worldview and traditions that restore humanity to a healthier state of living alongside our non-human relatives in a way that merges these two; the current,

Christianized state of understanding that fits our current paradigm and this animistic state of existing in the world that represents the paradigm we wish to create in the world. By taking a cue from our modern practices and conventions in their positive and relevant framing to present-day life, they become a keyhole through which to expand our perspective into the animistic, pagan pathways we are seeking with which to heal ourselves and our planet.

There are two significant folkways that have survived into modern-day Finland that help us and serve as a jumping point to create a fully realized, revived Finnish pagan spirituality. Those that are of particular interest to us here are the sauna (Finnish steam bath), and the *tonttu* (household/nature guardian spirits).

The Magic of Sauna

A tradition of sweat bathing has existed across many cultures throughout the world, but it is the Finns who have really put it on the map. Before we get any further, it's important that I tell you that you've probably been pronouncing "sauna" wrong. As a friend of mine recently said very succinctly, "sauna" is the only Finnish word that has become naturalized to the English language. As such, it should be pronounced the Finnish way. In Finnish, all of the vowels are pronounced. Always. So, the correct pronunciation is SAH-oo-nah, not SAW-nah. Sauna is common enough even within America that you can often find them at your local gym. There are even special infrared sauna centers popping up with cold plunge tanks for "contrast therapy" which, at the time of this writing, is one of the trending things in the fitness and wellness community. However, a dry, infrared sauna is NOT a traditional Finnish sauna.

Compared to our Nordic kin in native Finland, we have exceedingly few places we can go to indulge in true Finnish sauna therapy. In Finland, there is an estimated one sauna for every three people in the country. Apartments often come equipped with one, and upon arriving on their shores, a hospitable host will always offer a sauna right away. (And it's often considered somewhat rude to say no!)

So how does a traditional Finnish sauna differ from the one at your gym? To start, the most important aspect of a traditional sauna is the use of steam. In Finland, the steam is referred to as *löyly* which is also synonymous with the breath, vital life force energy, and is associated with the elemental forces of air and water. (*Löyly* is a very difficult word to pronounce for an American or English tongue, but if you pronounce it "LOW-loo," that's a pretty close approximation.) However, there are also other elemental forces present in the sauna for which it is customary in a ritual or healing sauna to be aware and reverent of: the fire in the stove, and the energy of earth within the wood being burned and the herbs used to create *vihta* (sauna whisks). *Vihta* are created by lashing together bundles of tree branches, most often birch, oak, juniper, ash, or sometimes maple. Different plants have different healing properties. For example, juniper is excellent for cleansing and purifying as well as being quite exfoliating. Birch is popular for its sweet smell and purification properties as well.

Traditionally, the sauna, not just as a ritual but also as a building, was incredibly important to the Finns, too. The sauna was often the first building erected on a new property or homestead. While other buildings were being built, it would function as a bedroom, bathing space, and kitchen. Culturally, the sauna was a place associated with transitions and rites of passage. There are specific rituals and spells centered around women giving birth in the sauna (where it was often the cleanest, most sterile location possible for such a delicate process), special sauna rituals for brides-to-be, and it was even a space where the elderly would go to die and/or have their body cleansed prior to burial or cremation. In between all of that, the sauna was where folk healers did the majority of their work through traditional healing techniques such as herbalism, bone-setting, cupping, massage, and energy work. Healers and sages would even divine meaning from the markings a good whisking with the *vihta* left on a person's back, or the shape and glowing of the rocks on the stove.

Unfortunately, not all modern people living in an English-speaking country have easy access to a sauna. However, the Kalevala itself actually gives us some insight into this challenge. There is a collection of runes about a character named Kullervo we can look to for guidance. Kullervo lives a fairly cursed life; having vowed while still in diapers to avenge the death of his family. While Kullervo had it way worse off than probably you or I, his feeling lost and out of place may be surprisingly relatable for diasporic Finnish-Americans or Finnish pagans trying to connect to this regional magic so far from its homelands. Kullervo is sitting and lamenting his poor fortune when he says,

...Others have their homes to go to,
To the comfort of their houses,
But my home is in the backwoods,
My estate is on the heather,
As my hearth is in the wind,
Sauna steam is in the rain.

—*The Kalevala: Rune 34, "Kullervo Finds His Family"*

Additionally, there is the very last rune of the Kalevala. Many scholars at this point agree this rune about Marjatta is likely a much more modern addition to the corpus of Finnish myth by Elias Lönnrot who, as a reminder, is the scholar and mythologist that compiled the runes into the Kalevala. Lönnrot was himself a proclaimed Lutheran Protestant, so the prevailing theory is that he wrote this story as a way to reconcile his fascination with Finnish-Karelian mythology and folklore with his personal Christian beliefs. Regardless of the reason for its writing, the Marjatta rune is a poetic and mythically relevant story. Within it, the chaste and virgin maiden, Marjatta, goes out to pick berries and one calls to her. When she eats the berry, she becomes pregnant with the Christ child. In a fascinating parallel to the story of Mary giving birth in the Bible, her parents refuse to let her give birth in the sauna because they assume she slept with someone out of wedlock. Without the support of her family, when she goes into labor, she sends her handmaiden to find a neighbor's sauna to give birth in instead. The handmaiden tries the neighbor, but they refuse Marjatta as well. The neighbor's wife says, "Where the whore of Hell may lie-in, bad one go to bear her child. When the horse blows out its breath, let her take her sauna there." In great distress Marjatta resigns herself to this and the Kalevala describes the experience:

When she got to the horse barn,
She besought the good horse meekly:
"Let your breath blow over me,
Puffing vapour on my belly;
Breathe out sauna heat to warm me
That this weak one may be strengthened,
For my need is very urgent"
Then the good horse breathed on her,
Draft colt breathes out in deep puffs,
Puffed out sauna vapour on her,
On the belly of the sick one.
Where the good horse huffed out heavily,
Vapour rose, as when thrown water
Hits the hot stones in a sauna.

—The Kalevala: Rune 50, "Marjatta"

Now, I promise I am not suggesting you go out and let a horse breathe heavily on you. (Although wouldn't that be quite the experience?) However, these passages do tell us that in a pinch, we have options. In the sauna, we find the components of the four elements of air (through the steam and smoke), fire, water (also from the steam and water poured over the stones), and earth (from the wood/herbs and the stones themselves). While an actual sauna is irreplaceable, we can draw on these original ingredients and myths to create small, similar rituals that can help us feel more connected to the magic of sauna in the absence of the authentic experience.

Approximately 90% of modern Finns take a sauna at least once a week. Unless you are very lucky, you may be hard-pressed to find the time and opportunity to visit a sauna so often. So, for you, dear reader, I have created this Shower Purification Ritual to help you connect to this gentle, ancient magic. You may do it as often as you shower, monthly or weekly as a special ritual, or however often you would like. I have also included, wherever possible, multiple iterations of including each element. While you should certainly aim to include at least one component from each element, you shouldn't feel obligated to use all of them every time if you don't have all the materials or energy.

Shower Purification Ritual

Supplies:

- A sprig or branch of dried herb for burning (juniper or birch are traditional, but others can suffice.)
- A lighter
- Fire-safe container
- A small bundle of birch twigs with leaves attached (a nice alternative is eucalyptus)
- A large bowl of fine sea salt (1–2 cups)

Arrange all your supplies on a secure, safe, flat surface. Undress completely and take a moment before beginning to focus on your intention in this ritual. Your shower ritual is intended to purify and cleanse your physical and energetic body. Additionally, this ritual is intended to help connect you to the deep ancestral roots of steam bathing. Hang your small birch (or eucalyptus) bundle from the shower head before you start.

Bow your head in thanks to the spirit of the plant. You may say a word of thanks if it feels good to do so. Take your lighter and do the same; bow your head and give thanks for the spirit of fire in this space. Light your dried herbs and smoke cleanse every corner of your shower and bathroom. Once you've done that, place the herb into your fire-safe container and allow it to continue smoldering until completely burned, if you can do so safely. (Otherwise, smother it to extinguish it before moving forward in the ritual.)

Now, turn on the water in your shower as hot as you are able to. Sit outside the shower and allow the steam to begin to fill the space. Feel the steam and the heat soaking into your skin. Take a few moments to thank the spirit of the water for its cleansing and purification. Thank the spirit of the air in the steam for filling your lungs and giving you life. Say simply, "*Terve, Löyly.*" (Pronounced "TEHR-vey, LOW-loo," meaning "Welcome, Steam.")

When you feel ready, adjust the temperature as needed for comfort, and step into the shower. Allow the water to cascade down your back and let the heat melt the tension in your muscles.

After taking a few moments to relax into the water, hold your bowl of sea salt in your hands. Bow your head and give thanks to the spirit of the earth for being a part of this ritual with you. Take a handful of salt and begin to rub it all over your body. It should be exfoliating and invigorating. Once you've treated your whole body with the salt, rinse well with plain water.

After using the salt scrub and rinsing off, grab your whisk. Hold it in your hands and give thanks to the spirits of the plants that gave their lives so that you can participate in this ritual. Once you have finished your prayer, begin to gently slap up and down your body with it. Let your own comfort and pleasure be your guide to how hard or softly you apply your whisking. (It should not hurt, but it should be brisk and enjoyable.)

After this, you may choose to stay in the water a bit longer and/or sit outside the shower in the steam. (You can turn the heat all the way up if you are no longer in the water and want to really crank up the steam.) Alternatively, you may enjoy turning the temperature down to be cool in contrast to the heat and steam for a few minutes before getting out.

Following the ritual, you may save your whisk to re-use if desired. Use your judgement as to when it needs replacing.

Household and Sauna Spirits

Another part of the sauna culture that has kept a foothold into the modern day is the *saunatonttu. Tonttut* (often translated in English to mean "elf" or "elves") are guardian spirits that attend to and protect various buildings on the homestead. While most *tonttu* were expected to be small in stature, cleanly dressed, and usually wearing a pointed red stocking cap, the sauna *tonttu* was most recognizable because they were entirely covered in soot and ash. This harkens back to a time when the most common form of sauna in Finland was a *savusauna* (smoke sauna) which had no chimney and the smoke was allowed to completely fill the structure while the stones were being heated. Only after the stones got warm would the fire be extinguished and the smoke let out. Naturally, *savusaunas* were quite sooty and, therefore, so was the *saunatonttu.* Usually, *tonttut* were believed to be incredibly clean and well-kept, but *saunatonttut* were special; their dirtiness was often considered a point of pride. The *saunatonttu* was usually believed to either live in the loft above the sauna or between the sauna stove and the wall behind it. Even in the modern day, it has been a re-emerging part of popular culture to keep a small *tonttu* figurine somewhere in the sauna in honor of this long-held traditional belief. The *tonttu* would help to keep the sauna clean between uses and it is customary even today to leave enough *löyly* and heat in the stove behind for the *tonttu* to use after the family were done with their own steam baths. Of course, this does also have the very practical benefit of helping to dry out the wood of the structure after use as well.

While the *saunatonttu* are the part of this lore that has survived with the most longevity, the sauna was far from the only place that traditionally had these guardian spirits. Threshing barns, horse stables, and of course, the home itself, usually each had their own *tonttu* guarding them. Like their brethren in the sauna, these household spirits were also known to help keep the living and working spaces of the homestead clean and in good order, particularly at night after the family had gone to sleep. It was common to leave offerings for these guardian spirits weekly and at seasonal observances. The *tonttu* was, in some places, believed to be directly responsible for bringing wealth to the home, so the reciprocity of regular offerings was viewed as crucially important to a successful homestead and family life. It was also considered to be bad luck to interfere with the *tonttu's* tasks or try to sneak a peek at them by staying up through the night to catch a glimpse. A *tonttu* who felt its humans was meddling in their work was liable to abandon the household and its tasks altogether. One particularly pertinent tale that is told to children relates the story of a horse stable *tonttu* who, upon being slighted in these ways, not only abandoned the property himself but brought the prized horses belonging to the farmer with him! Suffice it to say, you want your *tonttut* to be on your side and not against you.

In a world that no longer pays homage to these helpful spirits, how do we re-forge relationships with these household beings? Sure, we can simply leave out offerings and hope for the best, but you may feel that something more ritualistic or intensive is in order, depending on where you live or how the property has been cared for in the past. In areas of Finland, Karelia, and Sweden, there was a similar creature that is often conflated with the *tonttu;* the *para.* This creature had a slightly more sinister twist to it. While it was often seen as the source of wealth in the household, this was because it was believed the *para* could travel to neighboring homesteads and farms to steal milk, butter, money, and/or corn. There was significant folklore connected to this being as a creature that a witch (*noita*) could conjure or create through magical spells. Granted, although these spells were often seen as somewhat diabolical depending on the context and incantations therein, there are examples of those that are done without a connection to the Devil that I have chosen to use as the inspiration for the *tonttu* invoking ritual spell I have included for you below. I will go into some details on the care and maintenance of your *tonttu* below. However, before you perform this spell, please keep in mind that, like any living, animate being, a *tonttu* must be cared for. To invoke or conjure a *tonttu* is a commitment. The folklore tells us that to insult or mistreat a *tonttu* can lead to great misfortune. So, do not perform the spell below unless you are prepared to enter into a relationship of reciprocity with this household spirit.

Tonttu Conjuration Spell

This spell can be performed at any time, but the ethnographic and folkloric records show that it was commonly done during special occasions such as the night before Joulu (Christmas), or Midsummer. Certainly, these are particularly potent and powerful liminal days for conjuring a spirit. However, you should use your discretion as to what feels best to you. The best opportunity for this ritual is to do it during a ritual purification shower or sauna session. The sauna, as previously mentioned, was viewed as a liminal space between life and death; the access to the Spirit World was especially easy in this place. Likewise, "birthing" or conjuring a household spirit in this way holds great power and potency. So, in addition to the supplies needed for a ritual purification shower you will also need:

- A palm to fist-sized stone
- A bowl of rainwater
- A bowl of milk or cream

1. Take all the time needed to find the right stone for your conjuration spell. It should be a good-sized rock. You will end up placing it on a shrine after the ritual, so let that help dictate the size you pick.

2. When performing the smoke cleansing portion of your ritual shower, also smoke cleanse the rock you've chosen to use as a fetish.
3. Next, drip the rainwater onto the stone. It is believed that rain comes from the great god, Ukko, and creates animacy; bringing things alive and into reciprocity with humans.
4. Hold the *tonttu* fetish stone in your hands. Hold the fetish between your knees or in front of your lower belly and repeat the following incantation nine times:

ENGLISH:	FINNISH:
Tip-toe tonttu, deeply dreaming,	*Talon tonttu, tulen tuntija,*
Here now healing, silent scheming	*Päivän peitossa paranen*
Partnered promise, here pertains	*Anna lupa luoda, liittyä*
Honored home, here now remain	*Koti alla kurkihirren*
Birthed and beckoned,	*Tule, tulisijan suojelija*
partner mine	*Nosta oma onnemme ylös*
Luxury, luck, and largesse find	

5. After completing your ritual shower, find a place of honor where you can keep your *tonttu* fetish. Directly following the ritual, leave it an offering of milk or cream. After 24 hours, dispose of the offering in nature, safely.

The Care and Feeding of Your Tonttu

Tonttut are prideful creatures who appreciate consistency and punctuality. After you've established a good relationship with them, there is some room for grace if you forget a week's offering or slip up in some other way. However, their patience may be thin, and building strong trust in a relationship early on is crucial in any budding friendship. After the initial offering, you should plan to make an offering at least weekly to your *tonttu.* Gruel or oatmeal is traditional. Coffee or tea are common offerings for my own household spirits. As you dive deeper into your practice, you'll want to start paying attention as your *tonttu* may want particular things as offerings. These things may come to you in dreams, or perhaps a gentle whisper at the edge of your hearing, or even a flash of a vision that you may be tempted to assume is a figment of your imagination. Listen to these little messages. This is how spirits speak, and you certainly don't want to miss any requests from your *tonttu*. It is better to give too much than not enough, after all. Additionally, it is very important to acknowledge your *tonttu* on feast days and seasonal observances.

It is polite and typical that any offerings, especially offerings of food or drink, are portioned out before any other plates or portions are taken by humanfolk. In addition, these offerings might also include things like bread, beer, milk, cream, fish, etc. Whatever you are yourself feasting on (even if it is not traditional Finnish food) is what your *tonttu* will be grateful to have. There is also a custom at Christmas time that the leftovers from the holiday feast would be left out on the table overnight as it was the one time of year that the *tonttu* would gorge themself to the point of nearly exploding. Christmas Eve was the *tonttu's* annual dalliance into overindulgence, contrasting the usual where *tonttut* are incredibly reserved and responsible. Offerings may be left at a shrine if desired. Other common places to leave offerings to household spirits are at a special tree or flat stone outside the home or associated building as well. I like to think that the *tonttu* appreciates a warm, cozy spot to enjoy his gifts, but if you are still and listen closely enough, they will tell you precisely where and what they want.

Final Thoughts

These three facets—learning to work with raising your personal power (*luonto/lempi/vitun-väki*), studying and experiencing the magic of the sauna, and developing a relationship with your local household spirits (*tonttu*)—are just the beginning of creating a beautiful Finnish folk magic practice. Dedication and commitment to these traditions can form a seed which I hope to be able to help you continue to nurture. However, right now it looks like your coffee cup is quite empty, and the fire in the stove has burned down. The *pulla* is just crumbs in your lap and your eyelids seem to be growing heavy. I know we have covered a lot, my friends. It is time for you to let your mind rest. Rest now, and may the slumber of the sages fall upon you tonight; the type of sleep that takes these amorphous shapes of ideas and information and forms them into practice and understanding. When day breaks again, I pray you'll pay me another visit. There is still so much more to talk about; so much more magic I wish to share with you. But just for today, thank you for being here. Thank you for listening to the wisdom of these Old Ways. May they bring you peace and connection to the ancestors. *Voimaa ja valoa.* (Strength and light.)

Bibliography

Kunnas, Mauri. *The Book of Finnish Elves.* Otava Publishing Company, Ltd. Helsinki, 1979 (English translation by Tim Steffa, 1999).

O'Kelly, Emma. *Sauna: The Power of Deep Heat.* Welbeck Balance, 2023.

Sarmela, Matti. *Atlas of Finnish Folklore.* Suomalaisen Kirjallisuuden Seura, 2009.

Siikala, Anna-Leena. *Mythic Images and Shamanism: A Perspective on Kalevala Poetry.* Finnish Literature Society, 2002.

Stark-Arola, Laura. "Lempi, Fire and Female Väki: An Exploration into Dynamistic Relationships in Finnish-Karelian Magic and Folk Belief." *Journal of Ethnology and Folkloristics,* vol. 5, no. 2, 2011, pp. 34-55.

Stark, Laura. *The Magical Self: Body, Society and the Supernatural in Early Modern Rural Finland.* Finnish Literature Society, 2006.

Toivo, Raisa M. *Faith and Magic in Early Modern Finland.* Palgrave Macmillan, (2016).

Permissions Acknowledgements

"Everyone's Got a Haunted Barn: Ozark Daemonology in Practice" by Brandon Weston. First published in the United States in *The Crow's Collection Anthology: World Magic*. Copyright © 2025 by Brandon Weston. Published by permission of the author.

"Burjeria Mexicana" by Laura Davila. First published in the United States in *The Crow's Collection Anthology: World Magic*. Copyright © 2025 by Laura Davila. Published by permission of the author.

"In Between Two Altars: Italian-American Folk Magic & Dual Faith Perspectives" by Frankie Castanea. First published in the United States in *The Crow's Collection Anthology: World Magic*. Copyright © 2025 by Frankie Castanea. Published by permission of the author.

"Living the Sacred Calendar: Spiritual and Magical Practices of the Contemporary Maya" by Kenneth Johnson. First published in the United States in *The Crow's Collection Anthology: World Magic*. Copyright © 2025 by Kenneth Johnson. Published by permission of the author.

"Journey in Ocha: The Mysteries of Lukumí" by Oracle Hekataios. First published in the United States in *The Crow's Collection Anthology: World Magic*. Copyright © 2025 by Oracle Hekataios. Published by permission of the author.

"Macumba and the Black Atlantic Tradition" by Nicholaj de Mattos Frisvold. First published in the United States in *The Crow's Collection Anthology: World Magic*. Copyright © 2025 by Nicholaj de Mattos Frisvold. Published by permission of the author.

About the Contributors

Aili Marjatta Kerttula

Aili is a fourth-generation Finnish-American immigrant who has been a practicing pagan witch for 20+ years. A self-described "armchair scholar," Aili is a lifelong learner of everything related to magic, mythology, and animism. She has spent her entire life fascinated by her Finnish heritage and dreams of sharing the entrancing world of Finnish magic and folklore with the modern Neo-Pagan and occult communities. Aili is currently working on her own book that explores the practical application of Finnish ethnographies and folklore to create a modern, spiritual folk magic practice aligned with the seasons, the elements, and nature.

Brandon Weston

Brandon Weston is a folklorist and writer living in the Arkansas Ozarks. He is the author of *Ozark Folk Magic: Plants, Prayers, and Healing*, *Ozark Mountain Spell Book*, and *Granny Thornapple's Book of Charms*. He is the owner of Ozark Healing Traditions, a collective of articles, lectures, and workshops focusing on traditions of medicine and magic from the Ozark Mountain region. He comes from a long line of Ozark hillfolk and works hard to keep these traditions alive for generations to come.

Frankie Castanea

Frankie Castanea, also known as Chaotic Witch Aunt, is a practicing folk witch. They have been on a journey of reconnection to culture and ancestral practices for almost four years now, and within it have found a passion for sharing their ways with others. They are the author of *Spells for Change* and the upcoming book *Ancestral Magic* (2025). They read tarot and Italian playing cards professionally at Ritualcravt in Wheat Ridge and enjoy reading a variety of books in their down time.

Katerina Sarpione

Katerina Sarpione is a sorceress based in Bulgaria, dedicated to preserving and sharing the rich traditions of her land. With over 20 years of experience in the occult, she explores the ancient magical practices and folklore of the Balkans, blending historical knowledge with contemporary insight. Katerina believes the wisdom of the past lies not just in its rituals but in understanding their deeper meaning, making them relevant to modern life. For her, magic is intertwined with life itself, offering wisdom to those willing to look beyond the surface and connect with its truths.

Kenneth Johnson

Kenneth Johnson has published many books. His best-known works are *Mythic Astrology* (co-authored with Arielle Guttman), a vast reference work on the archetypal symbolism which lies behind all the planets and signs used in astrology (and still in print after 29 years), as well as *Jaguar Wisdom: An Introduction to the Mayan Calendar*—carried through Latin America by gringo travelers for many years now, right next to their Lonely Planet guidebooks. His works have been translated into German, Portuguese, Japanese, Czech, Russian, and Bulgarian.

Laura Davila

Laura Davila is a fifth-generation Mexican witch, a long-time practitioner of Mexican ensalmeria, hechicería, brujeria, and folk Catholicism. Born and raised in Mexico, Laura has lived in the US since 2010. Laura identifies as a "bruja de rancho"—a "ranch witch"—a term with great resonance in Mexico indicating knowledge of botanicals and the natural world. She learned her practice at her grandmothers' knees. Laura is also a Tarot card reader and a flower essence practitioner.

Nicholaj de Mattos Frisvold

Nicholaj de Mattos Frisvold graduated in psychology, anthropology of religion, and cinema studies at the University of Oslo and NTNU, Trondheim, Norway. He is the owner of Sacred Alchemy Store and the retreat center The Monastery of St. Uriel, Archangel. He has been living in Brazil since 2003 where he has dedicated much of his time studying, both as a practitioner and as an ethnographer, the varieties of Brazilian spirituality and sorcery.

Oracle Hekataios

Oracle Hekataios (he/they) is an interfaith minister, teacher, and author. Initiated into multiple traditions of the Craft, he recently began his personal journey into Lucumí. A priestx of Hekate and Dionysos, his passion is in philosophy, occult history, and theology. He lives in Florida.

P. Sufenas Virius Lupus

P. Sufenas Virius Lupus is a metagender person, practicing a queer, Graeco-Roman-Egyptian syncretistic reconstructionist form of devotional polytheistic mysticism dedicated to Antinous—the deified lover of the Roman Emperor Hadrian—and related Deities and Divine Beings. E is also in divine/spirit marriages with the Greek Goddess Thetis, a Mountain, and a formerly-living Wolf. A former professor with a Ph.D. in Celtic Civilizations, e practices a Celtic Reconstructionist methodology, utilizing form of polytheism in the traditions of *gentlidecht* and *filidecht*, amongst eir other involvements in several religious traditions. PSVL continues to teach courses in these (and other) subjects to modern polytheists interested in taking them. Lupus's poetry, fiction, and essays have appeared in many esoteric, Pagan and polytheist periodicals and anthologies. Lupus has also written several monographs, including *Ephesia Grammata: Ancient History and Modern Practice* (2014) and its ten-year anniversary expanded edition (2025), with more on the way. Lupus can be found online at http://psufenasviriuslupus.wordpress.com/.

Rain Al-Alim

Rain Al-Alim is a practitioner of *rūḥāniyya,* or Arabic spiritual magic, and an independent researcher in the field of Islamicate Occult Sciences. His journey began as a student of a local Turkish spiritual healer (*hodja*), after which he continued his studies with different teachers and magicians from across the Islamic world. He is the author of *Jinn Sorcery*, a compilation of English translations of various jinn summoning operations. Over the years, he has gathered a rich collection of occult manuscripts and texts in Arabic, Persian, and Ottoman Turkish, which he is currently translating and studying as part of his ongoing personal research projects.